Andrew William Kerr

Scottish Banking During the Period of Published Accounts,

1865-1896

Andrew William Kerr

Scottish Banking During the Period of Published Accounts, 1865-1896

ISBN/EAN: 9783337114350

Printed in Europe, USA, Canada, Australia, Japan

Cover: Foto ©Suzi / pixelio.de

More available books at **www.hansebooks.com**

SCOTTISH BANKING

DURING THE PERIOD OF
PUBLISHED ACCOUNTS

ABERDEEN UNIVERSITY PRESS.

SCOTTISH BANKING

DURING THE PERIOD OF

PUBLISHED ACCOUNTS

1865-1896

BY

ANDREW WILLIAM KERR, F.S.A., Scot.

AUTHOR OF "HISTORY OF BANKING IN SCOTLAND"

LONDON
EFFINGHAM WILSON
11 ROYAL EXCHANGE, E.C.
1898

TO

Monsieur GUSTAVE FRANÇOIS,

DOUAI, FRANCE,

IN RECOGNITION OF

HIS EVER ACCURATE AND APPRECIATIVE

EXPOSITIONS OF BRITISH ECONOMIC INSTITUTIONS

TO CONTINENTAL READERS,

AND

AS A TOKEN OF LONG-CONTINUED

PERSONAL FRIENDSHIP AND ESTEEM,

THIS VOLUME IS DEDICATED

BY

THE AUTHOR.

PREFACE.

THE principal portion of the following pages was recently contributed to the *Glasgow Herald* as a series of articles entitled "Thirty Years of Scottish Banking". These articles are now, through the courtesy of the proprietors of that influential journal, republished in collected form, after revision, together with the statistics and other data on which they were based; in the hope that they may be useful to members of the banking profession and to others who are interested in economic subjects. If the information annually supplied by the banks in their reports is to be properly utilised, it is necessary that retrospects be taken from time to time; so that, by contrast of period with period, the value of past policy may be accurately gauged.

The writer is fully conscious of the deficiencies of his execution of this work; and he will rejoice to see his essay supplemented by competent students of banking experience. He has, however, the satisfaction of feeling that he is placing within easy reach, a large amount of (hitherto practically inaccessible) material for the careful and detailed study of that system of banking to which the prosperity of Scotland is greatly due, and which receives world-wide notice in general banking discussions. It is only by such study that the benefits of experience can be fully obtained; and that reasonable hope of a perpetuation of past success can be secured. Each man's experience comes, for the most part, too late for him to derive the full advantage of it himself. But he can counterbalance this by availing himself of the experience of past generations. There is nothing new in the principles of banking, nor in their application. The changes are all in details and in the conditions of the business world. Owing to extended transactions, subdivisions have become more complicated; while, with the growth of population and wealth, the general business world has assumed more active and competitive aspects. But the experience of the banker of 1865, rightly read, is as valuable to-day as it was to the men of his own time.

I do not seek more, for this small work, than that measure of appreciation in use which has attended my two former efforts for the benefit of Scottish banking. It is now twenty-three years since I initiated the movement which, by the influence and exertions of a few large-minded bankers, was successfully accomplished by the inauguration of the Institute of Bankers in Scotland, which I was privileged to take an active part in organising. But I did not then contemplate that the movement would have such widespread acceptance as to extend, as we now find it, not only throughout Scotland, but to London, the provinces of England, the Australian Colonies, and the Dominion of Canada. My *History of Banking in Scotland* was the outcome of a conviction that the students of the Institute, while supplied with economic, law and other text-books, had no means of systematic study of the history of their profession; and I have had the gratification of knowing that it has been in constant use. I hope that my present labours may also be found to fill a vacant niche in banking libraries.

Advantage has been taken of the present republication, to discuss a few minor points which, while not usually referred to in the public consideration of banking affairs, are yet of vital importance to a just estimate of conditions in which man's relationship to man is a primary factor.

A. W. K.

CONTENTS.

CHAPTER		PAGE
	Preface	vii
I.	Characteristics of the Period	1
II.	The General Position	14
III.	Individual Experience	32
IV.	Profit and Loss	42
V.	Provision for Losses	82
VI.	Bank Note Issues	86
VII.	The Ultimate Gold Reserve	92
VIII.	Evolution	103
IX.	Arrangements and Functions	111
X.	Bank Agents	128
XI.	Bank Officers	135
XII.	Staff Aspects and the Institute	141
XIII.	Company Auditing	153
XIV.	The Death of Companies	158
	Appendices	165
	Index	171

SCOTTISH BANKING DURING THE PERIOD OF PUBLISHED ACCOUNTS.

CHAPTER I.

CHARACTERISTICS OF THE PERIOD.

BANKING in Scotland is so intimately associated with the upbuilding of the country's prosperity, that it may be regarded as a national institution, deserving and requiring periodical inquiry as to its methods and procedure, in the interests both of the proprietors of the banks and of the public. In order to accomplish this satisfactorily, it is necessary not only to examine from year to year the position of the banks, but likewise to review, at suitable periods, the course of the banking business, and to inquire how each establishment has fared in relation to the general experience. The consolidated character of the Scottish banking system, and the uniformity of practice of the several banks, make such inquiries both more necessary and more readily accomplished. The completion of a period of thirty years since the banks generally adopted the practice of publishing their accounts, presents a suitable opportunity for making such an examination at the present time.

It was in the year 1865, when the acuteness of the crisis accompanying the failure of the Western Bank of

Scotland had passed, but while the impressions made by it were still vivid, that the banks in Scotland first generally adopted the practice of publishing annual reports, with abstract balance-sheets and profit statements. Some of them had, indeed, previously given more or less information to the public; the younger banks being generally less reticent than their older rivals, who jealously preserved the secrets of the prison-house. The banks in Glasgow published their yearly statements in the newspapers for several years before those in Edinburgh did so. The first of the latter to follow the example was the British Linen Company. Of course, the dividend was always an index to the profits. But in regard to the general state of the banking business, and the relative positions of the several banks, there was almost absolute ignorance, or at best only shrewd guessing. The advent of the reports was therefore received with a large amount of interest, and no few surprises, by bankers and the public.

At that time the banking system of Scotland consisted of twelve independent banks, all exercising the right of issue, with 682 branch offices. These were, in the order of their formation: the Bank of Scotland, the Royal Bank of Scotland, and the British Linen Company (which may be conveniently considered as the old banks), the Commercial Bank of Scotland and the National Bank of Scotland (the new chartered banks), the Aberdeen Town and County Banking Company, the Union Bank of Scotland, the Central Bank of Scotland, the North of Scotland Banking Company, the Clydesdale Banking Company, the Caledonian Banking Company and the City of Glasgow Bank. The Central Bank was absorbed by the Bank of Scotland in 1868, the City of Glasgow Bank failed in 1878, and the other ten banks are still carrying on business. All, however (except the three old banks), have altered their constitutions, and some their names (besides assuming the word "Limited"), in connection with their registration with limited liability under the Companies Acts, as a consequence of experience of the results of unlimited responsibility of shareholders.

BANKS' EXPERIENCE AS PER THEIR REPORTS.

1865. Highly profitable results (Union). Period of unusual anxiety in banking affairs (Clydesdale).
1866. Good rates and increasing business (T. & C.). Continued depression of consols (B. L. Co. and N. of S.).
1867. Exceptional profits (B. L. Co.). Profits exceptionally large (Commercial). Unusually low rates for money (T. & C.). Reduced value of money (Clydesdale). Low rates (N. of S.).
1868. Rates of interest have continued low (N. of S.). Depression (City of G.).
1869. Depression in investments (T. & C.). Improved value and demand (Clydesdale).
1870. Extensive bill forgery. Low rates and dull trade (B. of S.).
1871. Appreciation of investments (T. & C.), (N. of S.). Extra and incidental profits (National). Recoveries (Clydesdale).
1872. High value of money (Clydesdale), (Caledonian).
1873. Special bad debts and defalcations (B. L. Co.).
1874. Bad debts exceptionally large (Union). Value of money lower and more bad debts (Clydesdale).
1875. Collie frauds (Union). Special bad debts (Clydesdale). Industrial stagnation (B. of S.).
1876. Continued depression in trade (Royal). Trade depressed (B. L. Co.). Dull trade, cheap money (Clydesdale). Profits narrow, business contracted (N. of S.).
1877. Low value of money, losses unusually small (National). Low rates (Union).
1878. Low rates (Royal). Steady business, small losses (National). Over average bad debts (Clydesdale). Excellent harvest (N. of S.). Failure of City of Glasgow Bank.
1879. Low value of money, small demand (National). Bad debts (N. of S.). Stoppage and losses (Caledonian).
1880. Rates unusually low (B. of S.). Improvement in business (Commercial). Moderate profits and losses (National). Improved business (Clydesdale). Low rates (Union).
1881. Profits better (B. of S.). Improvement in business (Commercial). Improvement (Clydesdale). Unfavourable experience (T. & C.).
1882. Better market (Royal). Profit on investments (B. L. Co.). Good demand for money (National). Good harvest, excellent fishing (N. of S.).
1883. Rates less remunerative but losses moderate (Commercial). Gross profits better but losses more (T. & C.).

1884. Depression (B. of S.). Stagnation (Royal). Continued depression (T. & C.). Increased trade demand for money (N. of S.).
1885. Depression (B. of S.). Depression prevailing feature (Commercial). Low margin of profits (Union). Depression (Clydesdale). Depression (T. & C.). Business moderately remunerative (N. of S.).
1886. Depression (B. of S.). Depression and low rates (Commercial). Diminishing demand (Union). Heavy losses (Clydesdale). Bad debts (N. of S.).
1887. Signs of improvement (B. of S.). Average value of money higher (Commercial). Fishcuring losses (N. of S.).
1888. Contraction of lending (B. of S.). Rate of profit higher but advances lower (Commercial). Fishing trade losses (T. & C.).
1889. Improvement (B. of S.). Business satisfactory (T. & C.). Rates low (N. of S.).
1890. Good demand for loans (B. of S.). Baring crisis. Sharp fall in prices of investments (N. of S.).
1891. Business well maintained (B. of S.). Business exceptionally favourable (Commercial).
1892. General dulness of business (B. of S.). Market unfavourable (National).
1893. Total absence of remark, but profits generally higher.
1894. Low rates and bad debts (B. of S.). Dundee crisis (Royal and Clyde.). Restricted demand and low rates (National).
1895. Profits moderate (B. of S.). Depression of trade and low rates (Union).
1896. Continuance of ease in money market (B. of S., April). Last quarter higher rates.
1897. Improvement of trade (B. of S., April).

A perusal of these reports is interesting, if only for the insight they give as to the causes that were supposed to be influencing the course of banking in Scotland. But in the main the compilers have erred on the safe side in saying too little rather than too much, and they have been most judicious in the avoidance of prophecy. The period embraced in our survey is particularly interesting, not only from the fact that we are enabled to study it with a much greater knowledge of its conditions than was previously possible, but also as being peculiarly typical, and exhibiting Scottish banking in its full maturity, and under conditions of as great prosperity and as great adversity as it had ever experienced. We have not, it is true, a complete record of bankers' views as to the series of years we are treating of, but from a careful collection of such remarks as to conditions of trade, money rates, bad debts, and relative points as are from year to year made in one or other of the reports, we gather a general opinion which is somewhat surprising. It is proverbial that farmers never have good weather, but few people will be prepared to find that the last generation of bankers have had very few favourable years. Of the thirty-three years—1865-97 inclusive—it would appear that only thirteen can be chronicled as good, even including those which were only deemed as " better ". The other twenty years, and they are not confined to the two last decades, are accompanied by such remarks as " interest rates unusually low," " bad debts exceptionally large," " mercantile failures numerous," " restricted demand for loans," " depression of trade," " industrial stagnation " (see Table of Experience). And yet the lean years did not swallow up the fat, but rather the fat the lean. Indeed, despite the woeful tale, the banks have fared well compared with other departments of business. Some of the establishments, perhaps, do not exhibit so prosperous an aspect as others, but this must be attributed to the incidents of individual experience.

But if the reports paint a blacker picture of the course of business in the country than is quite accurate, they are by no means singular in this. It is the fashion to talk as if diminished profits on the part of producers, distributers, etc., were synonymous with national adversity, notwithstanding the facts that consumers have been reaping the benefit of the low prices, and the vast majority of the population of the country is in a healthier, wealthier, and happier condition than had ever previously been dreamt of. In point of fact such lamentations are mainly one-sided, if not exaggerated. Capital has been steadily increasing at a greater ratio than the population, even if some wealthy men are somewhat less rich. The volume

POPULATION, TRADE, AND BANK PROFITS.

Year.	Population (Scotland).		Foreign Trade (U.K.).		Bank Profits.
	Number.	Increase.	Value.	Yearly Average and Rate of Increase.	Ten Banks.
1864	3,151,611		£487,571,786		
1865	3,181,383		489,903,861		£1,083,667
1866			534,195,956		1,135,202
1867			501,306,989		1,136,338
1868			523,100,229		1,037,180
1869			532,535,292		1,051,342
1870			547,430,820		1,055,511
1871	3,360,018	+ 6·61 %	614,235,869	528,785,100	1,086,323
1872			669,292,548	55 %	1,142,609
1873			682,292,137		1,246,312
1874			667,783,165		1,289,813
1875			655,551,900		1,254,519
1876			631,931,305		1,252,510
1877			646,765,702		1,269,605
1878			614,254,600		1,222,252
1879			611,775,239		1,095,060
1880			697,644,031		1,160,900
1881	3,735,573	+ 11·18 %	694,105,264	657,325.891	1,238,423
1882			719,680,322	24 %	1,237,522
1883			732,328,649		1,242,065
1884			685,986,152		1,195,837
1885			642,371,649		1,152,102
1886			618,580,489		1,175,165
1887			642,990,725		1,142,088
1888			685,520,979		1,140,937
1889			743,230,274		1,172,702
1890			748,944,115		1,212,689
1891	4,033,103	+ 7·96 %	744,554,982	696,413,833	1,239,557
1892			715,434,048	6 %	1,219,440
1893			681,826,448		1,256,182
1894			682,180,677		1,151,582
1895	4,152,115	+ 2·95 %	702,522,065	704,020,271	1,184,988
1896	4,182,868	+ 3·71 %	738,188,118	2 %	1,300,240
		+ 32·72 %		+ 54·74 %	£37,780,662
					19·99 %

of trade has greatly increased; and the value, though from 1875 to 1879 there was a falling off, has really been wonderfully good, showing an increase much greater than that of the population. Confirmation of this is found in the shipping returns, from which it appears that the registered tonnage of Scotland increased, between 1865 and 1893, by 180 per cent., while that of the United Kingdom increased by 52 per cent. Indeed, the Royal Commission on the Depression of Trade and Commerce seem to have had some doubt as to the reality of the depression, except in the agricultural interests. An examination of the declared profits of the banks shows that, all through the period with which we are dealing, they were wonderfully steady, with an overhead upward tendency. Of course, a very large increase in resources was steadily proceeding, in view of which such a result might be viewed as disappointing, if not unfavourable. Had the same ratio of profit continued, the profits would, of course, show a large increase in volume, probably to the extent of 50 per cent. But the decreased ratio of earnings is not due to depression in trade, but to the results of the large accumulations of capital, increased facilities for production, and accelerated means of transit, which have been developed to a phenomenal extent.

Of course we do not mean to say that the so-called depression is a phantasm. There has been a very real experience which has received that designation. But the designation is not quite applicable to the experience. Had it not been for the unquestionable depression in agricultural industry, the low value of money, the decreased profits as distinguished from the volume of trade, and the natural reaction from a period of "leaps and bounds," people would be congratulating themselves on the material prosperity of the nation. And even these unfavourable features, with a partial exception as to the first, mainly affected a comparatively small proportion of the population. Let any one look around, and ask himself the question, " What proportion of the population, under the rank of the middle upper classes, is in a worse position now as regards obtaining the necessaries and comforts of life than was the case thirty years ago?" and he will be bound to admit that the national prosperity has advanced enormously. But the classes have suffered while the masses have benefited.

Among the sufferers the banks will naturally be classed. But their adversity has been more negative than positive. The total declared profits are as large now as they were thirty years ago, even including the City of Glasgow Bank's return, which, as afterwards appeared, was quite unreliable. There has even been a realisation on the part of some of the banks of the expectation that the profits might keep pace in some measure with the increase of business, and, if all had been as steadily progressive as these, Scottish banking would have shown a very satisfactory, if not actually brilliant experience. It is not that some of the banks have profited at the expense of others. All have, apparently, had a material, although not equal, share in the expansion of business. But it does not appear that the ten talents have been more conspicuously successful than the five, or than the one talent.

But while we are disposed to take *cum grano salis* the complaints of the times being out of joint, it is undeniable that very adverse features have characterised the last two decades of banking experience. The banking advances have not expanded in proportion to the increase in deposits, and consequently a larger proportion of the banks' resources has been diverted into reserve securities, which of course are less remunerative. Moreover, it has been increasingly difficult to get suitable investments for surplus funds, the pressure for such being so great that the return on gilt-edged securities has been brought down to an unprecedentedly low point. But the chief adverse element has been the persistent downward course of interest rates. Thus while in 1864 and 1865 the cash account rates averaged 6·37 per cent., and the three months' discount rates for London bills averaged 6·09 per cent., in 1894 and 1895 the rates were 4·52 per cent. and 2·76 per cent. respectively. (Appendix A.) But this by no means exhausts the position. An increasing proportion of the advances is now made at special low rates; and the rates obtainable during recent years for floating balances in London have been almost nominal. The extent to which a bank's profits may be thus curtailed will be better realised when it is remembered that, while none of the Edinburgh and Glasgow banks has less than £10,000,000 of public liabilities, by a fall of ¼ per cent. on that sum, a reduction of £25,000 in the earnings would be sustained.

But, on the other hand, the banks have not sat still and paid away the old deposit rates while their lending rates were approaching zero. In 1864 the average deposit rates were as follows: Almost 3 per cent. on current account balances calculated daily, more than 4 per cent. on the minimum monthly balances, and little less than 4½ per cent. on deposit receipts. These rates were above the average rates of several preceding years; but, even allowing for this, they present a great contrast to present experience. Since then deposit rates have almost steadily fallen. In the ten years ending with 1875, the deposit receipt rate averaged only 2·67 per cent.; from 1876-85

2·54 per cent.; and from 1885-95, only 1·93 per cent. (Appendix A.) But it is not only by lowering rates that the banks have protected themselves, but also by the more radical method of discontinuing some of their interest arrangements entirely. On 1st July, 1885, the first step in this direction was taken by the abolition of the daily balance rate, all interest allowed on current accounts being thereafter calculated on the minimum monthly balances, the rate, at the same time, being reduced from $1\frac{1}{2}$ per cent. to 1 per cent. As it was generally supposed that under the latter system only about two-thirds of the actual balances bore interest, this would represent an actual interest payment of 13s. 4d. per cent. only. The old minimum of 2 per cent. on deposit receipts was also given up, and the rate reduced to $1\frac{1}{2}$ per cent. These arrangements held good for seven years and ninety-one days, during which time the current account rate remained at 1 per cent. But the continued pressure of low lending and investment rates at length necessitated a reconsideration of the position. A suitable modification of the situation might, perhaps, have been found by restricting the allowance of interest on accounts to those whose balances did not fall, during each month, below a fixed sum, such as £500 or £1000. But such an arrangement would probably have been only temporary, and a more drastic measure was adopted by the total abolition of the allowance of interest on current accounts. At the same time the deposit receipt rate was reduced to 1 per cent.; and, as an offset, the overdraft rate was reduced $\frac{1}{2}$ per cent. These changes took place on 1st October, 1892. The extent of the saving involved may be gauged from the statement of the chairman of one of the Edinburgh banks, that the changes made a difference to them of £30,000 per annum. It should be noticed, on the other hand, that various concessions have also been made from time to time in commission charges; but these are comparatively trifling.

The outstanding features of the period were the two crises of 1866 and 1878. The former—usually associated with the failure of Overend, Gurney & Co. for over £18,000,000—was more a mercantile than a banking crisis. Moreover, its effects were chiefly centred in England, Scotland being comparatively untouched. The Scottish banks experienced its effects only in the higher rates ruling for money. It was very different with the crisis of 1878. In that case the tornado concentrated its full force in Scotland, and proved to be one of the worst that had afflicted the country. The immediate cause, and outstanding illustration of the effects, of this exceptional crisis, are associated with the City of Glasgow Bank. The crisis would probably have occurred though that bank had never existed, but its manifestations would doubtless have been of a milder description. The unusual intensity of the calamity was fully realised by the banks. The striking illustration of the dangers of unlimited liability urged them to the protection of stockholders, and their responsibilities in the matter of maintaining their credit with the public received earnest attention. There appeared to be a consensus of resolution towards strengthening their positions. But good resolutions are proverbially evanescent; and it will be interesting and instructive to inquire how far the impressions of 1878 have had a lasting influence in the conduct of Scottish banking.

There was a semi-crisis in 1875, by which some of

the banks in Scotland were severely affected. It was mainly associated with the Indian and iron trades, and was focused in the failure of the firm of Alexander Collie & Co.; but was intensified by the fraudulent discounting practices of the senior partner of that firm, by which very heavy losses were entailed on bankers, the London and Westminster Bank being hit to the extent of £600,000, and the Union Bank of Scotland transferring £120,000 to provide for their share. In November, 1890, a periodic crisis occurred, which centred in the "personally conducted" liquidation of the foreign-loan banking firm of Baring Brothers & Co., whose acceptances were so largely held by the Bank of England and most of the other banking establishments of Britain, that, on the invitation of the former, a joint guarantee fund of many millions sterling was subscribed. Under this protection, the liabilities of the firm were assured, and its assets administered by the Bank of England. The liquidation extended from November, 1890, till early in 1895, when it terminated satisfactorily for all parties. No loss was sustained by the guaranteeing banks. The amount subscribed by the seven banks in Edinburgh and Glasgow was £300,000 each, or £2,100,000 in all. This incident was the subject of much criticism. If justifiable at all, the special treatment of Messrs. Baring was so only on the basis of special circumstances affecting other interests than theirs. It was a dangerous precedent, the justification for which would be applicable to numerous other cases, with the pernicious effect of encouraging dangerous business. But so far as the Scottish banks were concerned, they could not with dignity have held aloof when the leading English banks were supporting the Bank of England.

Among the notable events of the time, allusion must be made to the raid into England which was begun by the National Bank opening an office in London in 1864. Little notice was taken of that action, and even when the Bank of Scotland followed suit in 1868, slight opposition was shown by the vested interests of the metropolis. But when a third Scottish bank appeared in London in 1874, and more particularly when further intrusion was made by the Clydesdale Bank planting branches in Cumberland, a perfect tempest of indignation was raised against the Scottish invaders. Mr. Goschen appeared as an active champion of the English bankers, and introduced a bill in Parliament to enact that "the power of any banker to make or issue bank notes, whether in England or in Scotland, shall . . . be subject to the condition that such banker shall not . . . have any house of business or establishment as a banker in the other of the said parts of Great Britain". The bill was, however, withdrawn, and a proposal by Sir Stafford Northcote for a committee on the restrictions and privileges conferred by law on bankers in England, Scotland, and Ireland respectively, agreed to instead. A valuable blue book was the only tangible result. The banks, quietly but steadily, maintained their ground, with the result that opposition died out, the invasion was tacitly permitted, and the other Edinburgh and Glasgow banks were allowed peacefully, but not without bitterness of feeling, to follow into the metropolis in the wake of their brethren who had borne the burden and heat of the conflict.

CHAPTER II.

THE GENERAL POSITION.

In pursuing our inquiry into the progress of Scottish banking since 1865, the first point that falls to be considered is the growth of the business. And in order not to be restricted to a simple comparison between the positions as at present and in 1865, we propose to found also on the statistics of 1872 and 1883. The periods thus formed are irregular and arbitrary, but they are convenient, as the data for these years have already been tabulated in Somers's *Scotch Banks* and Kerr's *History of Banking in Scotland*. At the commencement of the period we are treating of, twelve banks were in business. These included the ten banks now existing, the Central Bank of Scotland (a small concern) and the City of Glasgow Bank. The former was absorbed by the Bank of Scotland in 1868, and the latter failed in 1878.

That the wealth of the nation is steadily increasing, not only in volume but in proportion to population, is proved by various taxation, financial, and commercial statistics. The figures relating to the growth of banking in Scotland are of the same tenor. The total liabilities of the twelve banks existing in 1865 amounted to £77,221,874. Last year the ten banks held funds to the extent of £124,259,067, showing an expansion of £47,037,193. The percentage of increase is 61, whereas the population, on a fair estimate of increase since last census, has increased by only 32·72 per cent. Or, to put it differently, while

TOTAL LIABILITIES.

Estab-lished.		1865.	1896.	Increase.	Per Cent.
1695	Bank - - - -	£8,709,725	£18,920,370	£10,210,645	117
1727	Royal - - - -	11,452,654	17,588,552	6,135,898	53
1746	British - - -	9,057,380	16,205,046	7,147,666	78
1810	Commercial -	9,471,155	16,811,377	7,340,222	77
1825	National - -	9,562,727	18,386,058	8,823,331	92
1830	Union - - -	9,834,605	14,235,357	4,400,752	45
1838	Clydesdale - -	6,402,704	13,194,194	6,791,490	106
1825	Town & County	1,574,510	3,159,346	1,584,836	100
1836	North - - -	2,314,527	4,340,908	2,026,381	87
1838	Caledonian - -	955,756	1,417,859	462,103	48
		£69,335,743	£124,259,067	£54,923,324	80
1834	Central - - -	1,177,444			
1839	City - - - -	6,708,687			
		£77,221,874	£124,259,067	£47,037,193	61

DEPOSITS.

Estab-lished.		1865.	1896.	Increase.	Per Cent.
1695	Bank - - - -	£6,488,227	£14,415,554	£7,927,327	122
1727	Royal - - - -	8,127,792	13,088,826	4,961,034	61
1746	British - - -	6,886,894	12,036,199	5,149,305	74
1810	Commercial -	7,088,835	13,542,638	6,453,803	91
1825	National - -	7,205,266	14,589,425	7,384,159	102
1830	Union - - -	7,771,887	11,443,482	3,671,595	47
1838	Clydesdale - -	4,578,710	9,743,930	5,165,220	112
1825	Town & County	1,221,655	2,471,081	1,249,426	102
1836	North - - -	1,716,128	3,362,359	1,646,231	96
1838	Caledonian - -	694,548	1,042,891	348,343	50
		£51,779,942	£95,736,385	£43,956,443	85
1834	Central - - -	954,134			
1839	City - - - -	4,446,365			
		£57,180,441	£95,736,385	£38,555,944	67

the average yearly increase of population during the thirty years has been 1·02 per cent., the banks' resources have expanded, on an average, by 1·97 per cent.—not very far from twice as rapid a rate. But the rate of increase of banking funds proceeded at a slower pace from 1883-96 than formerly, as also appears in regard to population.

The great volume of increase has been due to the deposits. These have been expanded from £57,180,441 to £95,736,385, a difference of £38,555,944, or 67 per cent. As we have seen, the inducement to depositors has been increasingly unfavourable. This finds its counterpart in the statistics now before us; for, whereas from 1865-72 the average yearly increase was £1,744,631, from 1872-83 it was only £1,240,571, and in 1883-96 it had fallen to £976,711. At first sight this result might seem to militate against the theory of the steady increase of national wealth. But this is not so. Owing to the discouragement necessarily given to depositors, the character of the deposit money has largely changed. The investment deposit which used to lie year after year undisturbed, except for interest calculation, is a thing of the past. Bank deposits are now funds *in transitu*, or, at best, awaiting a more favourable opportunity of investment. On the other hand, inducements to investors have multiplied greatly, and although good investment stocks command very high prices, the return on them is now, relatively to bank deposit rates, more favourable even than formerly. Still, in relation to population, an upward movement continues, for while in 1865 the deposits equalled £17 19s. 5d. per head, the figures were £20 8s. 7d. in 1872, £21 17s. 7d. in 1883, and £22 17s. 9d. in 1896. This is fully in accordance with the general theory as to increase of national wealth.

The course of the note circulation is interesting. The

banks' reports show an expansion of £2,306,568, or 46 per cent., which compares with 18 per cent. in 1883. Owing, however, to the mode in which the circulation is conducted under the Acts of 1844-5, it is necessary to take the Government returns to ensure accuracy of comparison. The average circulation for the year 1895-6 was £7,157,683, as compared with £4,361,256 (twelve banks) in 1864-5.

NOTE CIRCULATION.

	Per Reports.		Government Averages.			
	1865.	1896.	1864-5.	1895-6.	Increase.	Per Cent.
Bank	£553,160	£1,012,494	£493,078	£1,079,044	£585,966	118
Royal	*528,725	946,631	534,717	927,342	392,625	73
British	442,343	850,541	489,625	853,682	364,057	74
Commercial	697,425	972,625	555,227	929,454	374,227	67
National	679,075	861,180	472,094	827,044	354,950	75
Union	579,299	949,244	582,421	950,772	368,351	63
Clydesdale	408,170	858,381	373,026	715,651	342,625	92
T. & County	134,891	278,474	143,350	303,700	160,350	112
North	222,629	441,111	217,914	438,640	220,726	101
Caledonian	83,256	138,567	74,112	132,354	58,242	78
	£4,328,973	£7,309,248	£3,935,564	£7,157,683	£3,222,119	82
Central	53,310		61,443			
City	620,397		364,249			
	£5,002,680	£7,309,248	£4,361,256	£7,157,683	£2,796,427	64

Dates of Balance.—1896—27th February; 10th October; 15th April; 31st October; 1st November; 2nd April; 31st December; 31st January; 30th September; 30th June.

This shows an increase of £2,796,427, or 64 per cent. But when we compare the three consecutive decades of the thirty years, a varied experience is the result. For the first ten years the expansion proceeded at a much more rapid rate than subsequently. While in that decade the average yearly increase was £167,123, during the next

* Average for year.

ten years there was an actual decrease averaging £16,749 per annum. But the tide turned again during the next ten years, and the average yearly increase rose to £102,838. A further expansion occurred in 1895-6 amounting to £264,303, being less, however, than the increase during the preceding year. The explanation of these differences is probably that while the note circulation was a more active medium in the settlement of transactions than it subsequently became, the advancing prosperity of business caused an augmentation of the issues. Later, however, the banking troubles of 1878, involving the withdrawal of the City Bank issue, and the temporary suspension of that of the Caledonian, together with the increasing use of cheques, and other economies of cash payments, produced a large diminution of the circulation. But it is worthy of notice that the decrease had commenced before the crisis, the return for 1877-8 showing a fall of £191,235. The revival of activity in the circulation, during the last decade, is probably due to the continued increase of wealth and population, and has latterly been accentuated by the cessation of allowance of interest on current accounts. When customers began to realise that there was no advantage in paying into bank sums which they would shortly require, they adopted the practice of holding larger cash balances than formerly. While this active state of the note circulation is an indication of public prosperity, it is not an advantage to the banks. For not only do they derive no profit from the excess circulation beyond their authorised limits, but the additional expense entailed reduces the profit derivable from the authorised issues. It should also be noted that, in their own interests, the banks have, by improved exchange arrangements, endeavoured to keep the circulation at as low a point as possible.

The acceptances and drafts have increased by

ACCEPTANCES AND DRAFTS.

	1865.	1896.	Increase.	Per Cent.
Bank	£361,492	£1,333,759	£972,267	269
Royal	*378,576	709,168	330,592	87
British	276,501	423,459	146,958	53
Commercial	350,432	368,981	18,549	5
National	310,327	905,431	595,104	191
Union	231,023	169,008	‡62,015	‡26
Clydesdale	163,592	997,734	834,142	510
Town and County	—	—	—	—
North of Scotland	—	†20,401	20,401	204
Caledonian	—	†5618	5618	56
	£2,071,943	£4,933,559	£2,861,616	133
Central	—			
City	541,186			
	£2,613,129	£4,933,559	£2,320,430	99

CAPITAL SUBSCRIBED.

	1865.	1896.	Increase.	Per Cent.
Bank	£1,500,000	£1,875,000	£375,000	25
Royal	2,000,000	2,000,000	—	—
British	1,000,000	1,250,000	250,000	25
Commercial	3,000,000	5,000,000	2,000,000	66
National	5,000,000	5,000,000	—	—
Union	1,000,000	5,000,000	4,000,000	400
Clydesdale	900,000	5,000,000	4,100,000	455
Town and County	520,000	1,260,000	740,000	142
North of Scotland	1,600,000	2,000,000	400,000	25
Caledonian	500,000	750,000	250,000	50
	£17,020,000	£29,135,000	£12,115,000	71
Central	250,000			
City	870,000			
	£18,140,000	£29,135,000	£10,995,000	61

£2,320,430, or 99 per cent. over the thirty-one years. But this contrasts unfavourably with thirteen years ago, when

* Including sundries.   † Drafts only.   ‡ Decrease.

the total amount held was within £90,000 of what it is now. Indeed, were it not that 1896 showed an exceptional increase, the comparison would have been largely the other way. No doubt this is a reflection from the state of trade; but it results also from the growth in wealth permitting of cash payments to a greater degree than formerly. Economies in exchange arrangements must also have interfered with the use of letters of credit. The principal customers of the banks have now accounts with their bank's offices in London, Edinburgh, Glasgow, or other centre of their business transactions, by cheques on which the occasion for purchasing drafts is avoided. The falling off is, in the main, in the acceptances. The reports do not supply the data for making a comparison with 1865; but, taking the figures for 1878, the decrease in drafts is about £160,000, while the acceptances are lower by about £2,300,000. Moreover, this result appears to be caused by contraction in acceptances to banking correspondents, and not to mercantile firms. But there is considerable uncertainty in this item of the liabilities as supplied by the reports, the amounts being liable to great fluctuations owing to exchange settlements.

Together these several classes of the public liabilities show a growth of £43,182,939, or 66·64 per cent. While the banks' indebtedness to the public has expanded in so marked a measure, the aggregate addition to the proprietors' funds has been by no means inconsiderable. The paid-up capital, it is true, stands at a lower point than thirty years ago by £129,000. This is due to the disappearance of the capitals of the Central Bank and the City of Glasgow Bank, amounting together, in 1865, to £970,000, which has not been fully counterbalanced by increases of capital by the surviving banks. But if allowance be made for the fact that a considerable amount of the nominal capital of some of the banks was not in the hands of the public in 1865, but has since been placed, it will be seen that the apparent falling off is not real. The difference to be thus allowed for is probably about £850,000. But, if a decrease in the paid-up capital requires to be explained away, it is very different with the uncalled capital. Owing to the large additions made to subscribed capital in connection with the adoption of limited liability the increase in uncalled capital is very large, amounting to £10,995,000, or 61 per cent. Although this movement has not added strength to the position of the banks from a public point of view—the old system of unlimited liability having provided almost absolute security—it requires to be remembered in all questions relating to the security provided by the proprietors for their public liabilities. But whatever disappointment may be felt regarding the capital accounts, the reserved funds tell another tale. These show an aggregate improvement to the extent of £3,983,251, or no less than 133 per cent. That is to say, they are now more than two and a quarter times as large as they were thirty years ago.

This points to a considerable effort on the part of the banks to strengthen their position. But when we contrast the growth in the proprietors' funds with the growth in the public liabilities it is seen that the relative position is not nearly so strong as it used to be. In 1865 the aggregate proprietors' funds bore the proportion of 19 per cent. to the public liabilities. The proportion is now only 15 per cent. Only in one instance among the banks individually is an improvement in this matter shown. And in case it should be thought that the withdrawal of the Central and City of Glasgow Banks might explain or mitigate the position, it may be well to state that it so happens that the conjoined funds of these banks were almost exactly up to the average ; so that the existing banks show the falling off we have indicated from 19 per cent. to 15 per cent.

The first point to be noticed among the assets is the growth of the banking advances. These have increased from £54,849,854 to £67,942,250, or 24 per cent. Contrasting as it does with an increase of 66 per cent. in the deposits, this improvement is, of course, much less than might have been expected. It is apparent from the yearly reports that the banks have been unceasingly looking forward to a more active demand for banking accommodation. And, from time to time, as business or speculation moved the market, there seemed to be justification for hopes of improvement ; but disappointment invariably followed. No doubt a favourable experience will again be realised to some extent. But it may well be doubted if in the future profitable conditions comparable with those of former times will pay more than angels' visits—few and far between. People have more personal command of money than formerly ; and when they wish to supplement their private resources there is a much better market. The borrowers are becoming masters of the situation. Besides, it is probable that prices of commodities are permanently lower, and that the relative capital requirements will not be again on a scale equal to that of some years ago. When comparison is made between the periods 1865-83 and 1883-95, a great difference in

PERIOD OF PUBLISHED ACCOUNTS.

	Capital Paid up.			Reserved Funds.†			Total Proprietors' Funds.			To Public Liabilities. Per Cent.	
	1865.	1886.	Increase.	1865.	1886.	Increase.‡	Increase.	Per Cent.	1865.	1886.
Bank	£1,000,000	£1,250,000	£250,000	£306,846	£908,563	£601,717	£851,717	65	18	13
Royal	2,000,000	2,000,000	—	417,561	843,927	426,366	426,366	13	27	19
British	1,000,000	1,250,000	250,000	451,642	1,644,847	1,193,205	1,443,205	99	19	22
Commercial	1,000,000	1,000,000	—	344,463	927,133	582,670	582,670	44	16	13
National	1,000,000	1,000,000	—	368,059	1,030,022	661,963	661,963	48	17	12
Union	1,000,000	1,000,000	—	232,396	673,623	421,227	421,227	33	15	13
Clydesdale	900,000	1,000,000	100,000	352,232	594,149	241,917	341,917	27	24	14
T. & County	156,000	252,000	96,000	61,964	157,791	95,827	191,827	88	16	15
N. of Scot.	280,000	400,000	120,000	95,770	117,097	21,267	141,267	37	19	13
Caledonian	125,000	150,000	25,000	52,952	80,788	27,831	52,831	29	23	20
10 Banks	£8,461,000	£9,302,000	£841,000	£2,693,885	£6,977,875	£4,272,990	£4,924,990	44		15
Central	100,000			70,000			170,000		19	
City	870,000			230,000			1,100,739		17	
									20	
12 Banks	£9,431,000	£9,302,000	£129,000 *	£2,994,624	£6,977,875	£3,983,251	£3,654,251	29	19	

* Decrease, 1 per cent.   † Including dividends and balances.   ‡ 133 per cent.

experience is seen. During the former period there was an overhead expansion to the extent of 25 per cent., or an average of nearly £600,000 per annum. During the latter period there was an actual contraction of nearly £4,000,000, or 6 per cent. The downward course has not been quite continuous, having been considerably lower than the present point in 1888 and 1889—the difference being fully £2,500,000. The year 1896, moreover, has shown a general improvement.

As a natural consequence of the contraction in advances, the banking reserves have assumed very large proportions. The total amount of the investments, cash balances, etc., is £52,823,996, showing an increase of £31,561,839, or 148 per cent. This expansion, while a healthy feature as viewed from the standpoint of the public, is disappointing in an economic aspect. The old theory was that reserves should be about one-third of the amount of the public liabilities. Under modern conditions a higher proportion would probably be at all times advisable. But the present point of 48 per cent. is manifestly an unprofitable excess of strength. Indeed, the process has proceeded so far that the conduct of investment threatens to become as outstanding a department of the banks' business as their legitimate vocation of banking. The movement has been practically continuous throughout the period we are reviewing, and latterly it has been advancing with giant strides. Up to 1872 the increase was at the yearly average of £924,000, from 1872-83 at £952,000, and during the succeeding twelve years at £1,339,000. Should the contraction in advances and expansion in reserves proceed for five or six years at the same rate as recently, the investment portion of the operations of the banks will become, as regards volume, the more important of the two. Indeed, it may be a

BANKING ADVANCES.

	1865.	1896.	Increase.	Per Cent.
Bank	£5,488,607	£11,104,652	£5,616,045	102
Royal	8,206,985	9,657,392	1,450,407	17
British	5,926,964	10,197,474	4,270,510	72
Commercial	6,179,293	8,461,212	2,281,919	37
National	6,737,302	9,890,639	3,153,337	46
Union	7,507,748	6,844,803	*662,945	*9
Clydesdale	5,163,041	6,857,963	1,694,922	33
Town and County	1,182,032	1,663,389	481,357	41
North of Scotland	1,687,523	2,451,342	763,819	45
Caledonian	854,038	813,384	*40,654	*5
	£48,933,533	£67,942,250	£19,008,717	40
Central	1,103,512			
City	4,812,809			
	£54,849,854	£67,942,250	£13,092,396	24

BANKING RESERVES.

	1865.	1896.	Increase.	Per Cent.	To Public Liabilities. Per Cent.
Bank	£3,095,732	£7,215,673	£4,119,941	133	43
Royal	3,133,637	7,425,107	4,291,470	136	50
British	2,996,439	5,619,082	2,622,643	87	42
Commercial	3,192,242	7,900,205	4,707,963	147	53
National	2,724,159	8,055,519	5,331,360	195	43
Union	2,154,375	7,034,340	4,879,965	226	56
Clydesdale	1,140,315	5,889,794	4,749,479	416	51
T. & County	363,968	1,420,954	1,056,986	290	52
N. of Scot.	624,387	1,726,789	1,102,402	176	45
Caledonian	86,384	536,533	450,149	520	45
	£19,511,638	£52,823,996	£33,312,358	171	48
Central	57,270				
City	1,693,249				
	£21,262,157	£52,823,996	£31,561,839	148	33

practical question to consider whether the large banks may not require to devote more systematic attention to

* Decrease.

this increasingly important part of their business. Notwithstanding the care with which banks' investments are proverbially made, regularly organised departments for the conduct and supervision of the investments might be elements both of increased safety and of profit.

The last item among the assets that falls to be noticed is the heritable property accounts. These consist of the outlays on bank buildings, representing the value of the offices occupied by the banks for the conduct of their businesses, and accounts for heritable property yielding rent, consisting of houses, etc., which have come into the possession of the banks through foreclosure of mortgages, or been acquired for prudential reasons. Confining our attention to the bank buildings, the amount has, as might be expected, very largely increased during the thirty years. From £1,091,862 it has risen to £1,961,271, an increase of 80 per cent. (including the Central and City Banks, with 105 offices). This does not represent, however, nearly the total outlay, for it must be remembered that large sums are yearly laid aside to reduce the account. The total amount applied since 1865 to depreciation of real property is £911,162, of which almost all was on account of bank buildings. It will thus be seen that the actual expenditure has been about twice as much as the apparent increase. The amount written off may appear considerable; but when allowance is made for the fact that a large proportion of branch offices have cost much more than their local sale value, the 30¼ per cent. of depreciation must be deemed very moderate. And not only has the total expenditure been large, but the cost of the buildings would seem to have been considerably enhanced. Thus, while in 1865 the average amount in proportion to number of offices was £1573, in 1895 it was £1918, and in 1896, £1932. If the amount written off be included, as should perhaps be done, the latter sums will be £2751 and £2830. Of course this is a rough test, for we have not details of the number of offices owned by the banks, the businesses being sometimes conducted in rented premises. Besides, it is probable that a larger proportion of branch offices is now owned by the banks than formerly, thus tending to raise the average price. Still, it is hardly doubtful that the cost in relation to accommodation is higher now than it used to be. In treating of the expenditure on bank buildings, the cost of properties in London acquired in connection with the branches opened there is not included, except in the cases of two of the banks. The sum involved is £474,403, which is partly yielding revenue, but must be deemed as largely adding to the proper cost of bank buildings.

It is more difficult to deal with that portion of the real estate accounts which relates to rent-yielding property exclusively. Until after the crisis of 1878, it was not usual for the banks to give particulars of this item of their assets. And even now no particulars are given enabling an opinion to be formed as to the correctness of the valuations. Doubtless the original values were correctly enough ascertained, however, and the properties would not suffer from inattention to repairs. The sum at present represented by this item of the assets is about £1,000,000. But it need not be further differentiated from the bank buildings. The total amount of the heritable property accounts was £2,514,966 in 1879. At present it stands at £3,492,821, an increase of 34 per cent. Including what has been written off for deprecia-

| | *1865. | \multicolumn{5}{c}{Heritable Property.} | | | Bank Buildings. | |
		1879.	1896.	Increase since 1879.	Per Cent.	Written off since 1879.	Per Cent.	1865.	1896.
Bank	£125,386	£392,395	£600,045	£207,650	48	£178,000	23	£125,386	£233,798
Royal	112,032	434,509	506,053	71,544	16	61,683	11	112,032	247,987
British	133,977	252,317	388,490	136,173	54	155,000	28¾	123,977	240,401
Commercial	99,620	231,026	449,960	218,934	95	140,000	24	94,620	243,829
National	101,266	248,400	439,900	191,500	77	†25,729	5¼	101,265	§171,400
Union	172,482	359,135	356,214	†2981	†1	150,000	29¼	172,484	275,843
Clydesdale	99,348	339,830	446,436	106,606	31	109,500	19¼	96,348	§336,436
T. & County	28,510	63,150	75,004	11,854	19	46,750	38¼	28,510	66,504
N. of Scot.	2617	128,489	162,777	34,288	27	†22,000	12	2616	92,830
Caledonian	15,334	65,655	67,942	2287	3	22,500	25	15,333	52,243
	£890,572	£2,514,966	£3,492,821	£977,855	39	£911,162	20·69	£872,571	£1,961,271
Central	16,662							16,662	
City	202,629							202,629	
	£1,109,863		£3,492,821 79·31 of cost					£1,091,862	£1,961,271

* Bank buildings mainly. † Decrease. ‡ Special provisions made for depreciation. § Including London property.

tion, the total cost has been £4,403,983. It would thus appear that the property stands at about 80 per cent. of its cost price. As we have already indicated, sufficient data are not supplied to allow of a definite opinion being expressed as to the sufficiency of the provision for depreciation. But considering the somewhat unsaleable character of many of the branch buildings (which would be white elephants to the local tradesmen), and the very heavy fall which has taken place in the value of house property since 1880, 20 per cent. seems a moderate appropriation from profits.

The question of profits will be dealt with in a subsequent chapter, but there are a few other points which fall to be included in a review of the general position. In the development of banking the extension of branches has been a marked feature. In 1865, twelve banks had 694 offices; in 1872, eleven banks had 807 offices; in 1883, the presently existing ten banks had 912. The latest returns show the number to be now 1015. There were actually more branches (1021) open in 1894; but the reduction is entirely due to one bank, the Commercial. When it is remembered that even twenty years ago the extension of the branch systems was thought to have been overdone, this increase of more than ten offices per annum will be viewed as somewhat remarkable. Whether it has been as profitable is a question which will fall to be considered subsequently. Another noticeable feature is the great rise in the market values of the stocks of the banks which has taken place. From an average price of 196 per cent. for the twelve banks in 1865, the stock exchange quotations rose to 213 per cent. for the surviving banks in 1879, having, however, been as high as 286 per cent. during the preceding year. They rose again to 259 per cent. in 1884, and 308½ per cent. in 1897. The result

BANK OFFICES.

	1865.	1872.	1883.	1895.	1896.
Bank	61	76	107	118	118
Royal	75	93	126	128	128
British	53	61	104	119	119
Commercial	77	92	114	143	133
National	73	84	95	109	109
Union	105	113	125	134	136
Clydesdale	61	76	100	112	114
Town & County	32	34	52	63	63
North of Scot.	35	40	65	68	68
Caledonian	17	19	24	27	27
	589	688	912	1021	1015
Central	10	—			
City	95	119			
	694	807	912	1021	1015

PRICES OF STOCKS AND SHARES PER CENT. IN FEBRUARY.

	1865.	1879.	1884.	1895.	1897.	Increase or Decrease.
Bank	223	267	310	345	348	+ 125
Royal	162	183	217	222	228	+ 66
British	238	235	302	392	437	+ 199
Commercial	234	223	275	364	400	+ 166
National	218	244	307	344	393	+ 175
Union	185	175	222	210	230	+ 45
Clydesdale	193	176	225	198	210	+ 17
Town & County	178	257	242	303	305	+ 132
North of Scot.	200	266	271	231	240	+ 40
Caledonian	205	—	184	180	180	− 25
	200	213	259	288	308½	+ 108½
Central	250					
City	137					
	196					

is practically the same if the view be confined to the

existing banks. In their case the total value of capital stocks was about £17,000,000 in 1865; it is now nearly £28,750,000, although the increase of stock in the interim has only been £841,000. This result is not due in any great measure to increase of dividends; for although a few of the banks have made great strides in this respect the average rate has only risen from $9\frac{1}{4}$ per cent. to $11\frac{1}{5}$ per cent., being actually less now than it was thirteen years ago. The average return on the average price is 3·64 per cent. now, as contrasted with 4·72 per cent. in 1865.

From this survey of the course of banking in Scotland it would appear that while the growth of business has been remarkable as regards volume, the results have in several essential respects been disappointing.

CHAPTER III.

INDIVIDUAL EXPERIENCE.

MARKED as have been the movements shown by a survey of the aggregate experience of banking in Scotland during the last thirty-two years, the individual experience of the banks presents still more noticeable results. All the establishments have increased the volume of their businesses, but the degrees of progress have been various, the relative positions of the component members of the group have changed, and a great growth of business has frequently been accompanied by a comparatively unfavourable profit experience. Prestige has not sufficed to secure custom, nor has comparative weakness deterred public recognition. What economic laws have shaped the courses of banking experiences it would require much fuller information than statistics can supply to say. Questions psychological, and even physiological, moral and social, enter into the problem; and even the chapter of accidents, or what in our ignorance we have no better term for, has been potent to mould the destinies of our banking establishments.

The premier place as regards both increase and absolute amount of business falls to the premier bank.* The total liabilities of the Bank of Scotland have increased during the period under examination by £10,210,645, or 117

* See tables in chapter ii.

per cent.; and they now amount to nearly £19,000,000. Whereas at the opening of our period that bank only occupied the sixth place in respect of volume of business, it has now the first. It is, of course, the deposits which form the bulk of the liabilities, and in this department the Bank of Scotland shows a growth of 122 per cent.* It would appear as if it had got the lion's share in the portion of the City Bank's business. Next to it comes the Clydesdale Bank with an increase of deposits to the extent of 112 per cent.; but as this bank was comparatively small in 1865, the proportion of increase shows more largely than the actual amount, which is considerably exceeded by some of the other banks. Thus the National with 102 per cent. and the Commercial with 91 per cent. both show much larger increases in actual amount. The improvement in the case of the Commercial Bank since 1883 is conspicuous, and to a smaller extent the same remark applies to the British Linen Company. The Town and County and North of Scotland Banks show marked advances, the former having more than doubled, and the latter nearly doubled, the amount of their deposits. The other banks also show considerable increases, which are not, however, up to the general average. It is noticeable that the improvement in deposits has, except in the cases of the British Linen, Commercial and National Banks, been less rapid during the last twelve years than formerly. During 1896 the National Bank increased its deposits by the exceptional amount of £767,097, and now heads the list as the largest deposit-holder.

* The report issued last April shows no material change in the bank's position.

The remittance business shows marked diversity in the experience of the different banks. Thus while the Clydesdale Bank, the Bank of Scotland, and the National Bank all show a great extension of business, the Commercial has only an increase of 5 per cent., while the Union shows an actual falling off of 26 per cent. While several of the banks—the Royal, British Linen, Commercial, and Clydesdale—show extension of business in this department since 1883, those banks which have been most conspicuous for their cultivation of acceptance business— *viz.*, the Bank of Scotland and the National Bank—both show a contraction. But, perhaps, the basis for discussion of this subject is too uncertain to permit of satisfactory deductions.

Fortunately, in regard to the note circulation, we are on firmer ground, and from the Government returns of the average circulation a fair idea can be formed of the extent of public favour vouchsafed to each establishment. Not many persons, it is true, discriminate among the issues, and the extent of issues appears to be more nearly related to the number of branches than to the extent of the business. Thus we find that the Union, the Commercial, and the Royal, with the largest number of offices, headed the list until comparatively recently, when the Bank of Scotland stepped in front of them, and has since retained the leading position as regards supplying the circulating medium. This fact militates against the theory, for the Bank of Scotland comes fifth in number of offices. But it must be regarded rather as an exceptional circumstance than as an adverse argument. It would seem to suggest that the Bank of Scotland has a stronger hold on the industrial districts than the other banks, a view which finds support in its relatively greater progress in banking advances. The general average of increase for the ten banks is 82 per cent., and is only exceeded by four banks, viz., the Bank of Scotland, 118 per cent.; Town and County, 112 per cent.; North of Scotland, 101 per cent.; and Clydesdale, 92 per cent.; the Caledonian following with 78 per cent. This comparative activity of the provincial banks is remarkable, but may be due to less rapid exchanges than in the case of the Edinburgh and Glasgow banks. Including in the comparison the issues of the Central and City Banks, the increase in the aggregate circulation is 64 per cent., which is exceeded by all the banks except the Union, which is but slightly under it.

The place of honour in respect of additions to proprietors' funds has been secured by the British Linen Company, which shows an increase of £1,443,205. This result is mainly due to an issue of £250,000 of new stock, whereby a premium of £500,000 was realised; and to a previous issue in 1882 of stock which stood in name of the bank, the profit on which allowed £200,000 to be added to rest. But business profits have also borne a large part in building up the reserve fund, no less than £442,569 of the total increase having come from this source during the period we are reviewing. This large appropriation is only exceeded by the National and Union Banks, with the Commercial as a good fourth. The proportion of increase by the British Linen Company is 99 per cent. The Town and County Bank follows with an increase of 88 per cent. The Bank of Scotland, which made an issue of £250,000 of new stock in 1877, also shows the substantial improvement of £851,717, or 65 per cent. The only other bank exceeding the average of 44 per cent. is the National, with 48 per cent.; but the Commercial is pretty close at 43 per cent. The Royal has added £426,366 to reserve, and by reason of its large capital stands well in the proportion of proprietors' funds to public liabilities. It is, however, exceeded in this respect by the British Linen Company. As we have previously indicated, the banks do not hold so strong a position from this point of view as they used to do. There is only one exception to the general falling off, viz., the British Linen Company, and only other two banks, the Royal and the Caledonian, have not fallen below the average of 1865; while these and the Town and County alone maintain the present average of 15 per cent. The past year shows some notable additions to the reserved funds, the British Linen having added £100,000 (mainly from premiums on realised securities), the National £30.000, the Commercial and Union £25,000 each, the North of Scotland £17,500, and the Town and County £4000.

The experience as regards growth in banking advances is of a very diversified character. The Bank of Scotland has done very well with a growth of 102 per cent.—pretty nearly in equal ratio to the increase in total liabilities. The British Linen Company also has the fair increase of 72 per cent. The National, North of Scotland, and Town and County are also over average. But none of the others shows well; and the Union and Caledonian have actually contracted their advances. With the exception of the Bank of Scotland, British Linen Company, and Commercial Bank there has been a falling back within the last twelve years. The banking business is not keeping pace with the growth in resources, and there is an evident tendency towards becoming investment companies as much as banks. This is not a desirable movement, either from the banks' own, or from a public point of view; but there seems to be no help for it, unless the demand for accommodation greatly revives, of which the prospect seems remote. The reports issued during 1896 show a general improvement in the advance business, which is particularly marked in the cases of the British Linen and National Banks, while to a smaller extent the Commercial and Union Banks have also done fairly well. But, to a large extent, the increased advances are of a stock exchange, rather than of a commercial character. Of course the banks might discourage deposits, and so lessen the plethora of investment money, but their profits are not brilliant enough to permit of so self-sacrificing an action. Still, a steady increase of investments on the one hand, and of deposits repayable on demand on the other, is not in strict accordance with the economic position of banks, whose principal function is to fertilise the fields of trade and industry, and to lend capital on the double basis of personal and collateral security; maintaining always the liquidity of their assets. Besides, the more investments increase, the less liquid they tend to become. The adoption of the system of deposits for fixed periods would modify the economic objection, but it might increase the difficulty, by swelling the amount of borrowed capital.

The natural sequel to this experience is a striking growth in the banking reserves. Among the large banks the Union and the Clydesdale show the largest proportional increases—a feature which is somewhat remarkable. But there was considerable room for improvement from the rather low level occupied by them thirty years ago. They are followed by the National, whose reserves are nearly three times as large as formerly. The others all show large increases, varying from 87 per cent. on the part of the British to 147 per cent. by the Commercial. The north country banks, especially the Caledonian and Town and County, are conspicuous in the matter of enlarging their reserves. The Union Bank gives the largest proportion to public liabilities, *viz.*, 56 per cent. It is surely an abnormal position for a bank to hold more than half of its assets in the shape of investments and cash; and the case is the more remarkable, when it is that of the leading local bank of the commercial metropolis of Scotland, and having a larger number of branches than any of the other banks. The Commercial, the Town and County, the Clydesdale, and the Royal follow pretty closely above the general average of 48 per cent. The North of Scotland, the Caledonian, the Bank of Scotland, the National, and the British Linen graduate the list down to 42 per cent.

The heritable property accounts have been very variously treated by the different banks. Leaving out of account for the present the amounts which have been written off for depreciation, we find that the largest proportional increase has been made by the Commercial, which now holds nearly twice as much real estate as it did in 1879. This great addition is mainly due to London property, but bank buildings in Scotland have also added greatly to the account, which is natural from the large number of branches opened during the period. The Bank of Scotland and the British Linen Company have each increased their property by about a half, and the

National is not very far behind. But the actual amounts in the two latter cases are considerably smaller than with some of the other banks. Less has been done in the matter of providing for depreciation than might have been expected, the general average being only 20·69 per cent. of the full cost. The Town and County stands first with 38½ per cent., the Union being second with 29½ per cent., the British Linen, Caledonian, and Commercial follow with 28½, 25, and 24 per cent. The Bank of Scotland is not very far behind. Of the others, the Clydesdale alone has nearly attained the average. It is only just, however, to point out that both the National and the North of Scotland had, at an early period, made large provision for depreciation of bank buildings; consequently this comparison does not give full justice to them. Several of the banks carry £5000 yearly to credit of bank buildings account, and the latest statements show more than the usual attention to this matter, the National having written off £20,000 and the Bank of Scotland and Union Bank £10,000 each.

Branch extension has been a marked feature with all the banks, but while some were active in the earlier part of the period, and subsequently slackened their efforts, others reserved their energy for a later time. The Royal is a typical instance of the former policy, and the British Linen of the latter. Only the Commercial and the Clydesdale appear to have followed a steady policy in this respect. As it is, the relative places as regards number of offices have not altered in the thirty years so much as one would have supposed, although the differences are not so wide as formerly. That is to say that, generally, the banks having fewest branches in 1865 have opened most offices in the interim. But whereas the Union used to be distinctly first, the Commercial is now but little behind it, and the British Linen Company from being eighth is now fourth. Whether as a coincidence or as a result, the movement in these two cases has been accompanied by increased prosperity. But it should be borne in mind, that a strict comparison of proportionate increases from the number of offices previously open shows the progress to have been somewhat different, although even thus the British Linen Company comes out first. The two Aberdeen banks and the Bank of Scotland follow at some distance. The Commercial and Clydesdale are the only other banks over the average of 73 per cent. A careful study of the experience of the period does not show that prosperity and branch extension *per se* are co-related in any marked degree. This is confirmed by the somewhat unusual circumstance, in Scotland at least, of an extensive closing of branches, shown by the Commercial Bank last year.

The same feature of diverse experience meets us when we examine the relative prices of the stocks of the different banks. All, with the exception of the Caledonian (which has so bravely overcome unmerited adverse fate), show improvement, but the degrees vary from 199 per cent. to 17 per cent. Again the British Linen Company heads the list with an increase of 199 per cent., and holds the place of the highest priced stock, irrespective of dividend. The National and Commercial come next with rises of 175 and 166 per cent. The Bank of Scotland and Town and County with 125 and 132 per cent. are the only others which exceed the average increase of $108\frac{1}{2}$ per cent. The Royal shows 66 per cent., the Union 45 per cent., the North of Scotland 40 per cent., and the Clydesdale 17 per cent. The Caledonian Bank shows a fall of 25 per cent.

As a concise summary of this chapter, we subjoin a table showing the relative positions of the banks at the various dates with which we have been dealing, on the basis of a conjoined examination of the relative positions as regards (1) total funds, (2) proportion of proprietors' funds to liabilities, (3) subscribed capital, (4) banking reserves, (5) number of offices, (6) amount of net profits, and (7) proportion of dividend to proprietors' funds. In our next chapter we will discuss the profit and loss aspect of the banks' experience.

RELATIVE POSITIONS OF THE TEN BANKS.

	1865.	1872.	1883.	1895.	1896.	Better+ Worse -
Bank of Scotland	4	6	3	6	6	- 2
Royal	1	1	1	2	3	- 2
British Linen	5	5	7	4	4	+ 1
Commercial	2	3	4	1	1	+ 1
National	3	2	2	3	2	+ 1
Union	6	4	5	5	5	+ 1
Clydesdale	7	7	6	7	7	0
Town and County	9	10	9	8	8	+ 1
North of Scotland	8	8	8	9	9	- 1
Caledonian	10	9	10	10	10	0

CHAPTER IV.

PROFIT AND LOSS.

THEORETICALLY a banker should not make losses. All his advances should be so judiciously placed that repayment is certain. In practice, however, over-fearfulness of loss cripples business; and the banker who goes too much on the grip-for-grip principle finds his customers loth to trouble him. He, therefore, takes refuge in the insurance theory of averaging risks. Over a large number of small loans some danger may be profitably run. But the case is very different with large advances. Danger must, with them, be reduced to the irreducible minimum. An expert banker thus makes but a small percentage of loss over a series of years. The late Mr. Laurence Robertson's management was so excellent that, for ten years during the early part of our period, the total loss to the Royal Bank on advances averaged only 1s. 1¼d. per cent. per annum. On such a basis the total banking losses in Scotland should average at present about £35,000 per annum. It may be doubted, however, if in these latter days Mr. Robertson's experience is a common one—at least recent confessions are to a different tune. In any case, losses are to be expected, and must be provided for. It is, therefore, the practice, before declaring the profits, to make ample provision, year by year, for all accounts about which the slightest doubt is felt ; and, over and above, to build up a fund for unforeseen contingencies. This is irrespective of the reserve fund proper, drafts on which are only made as a last resort. There is, of course, no rule, either of principle or practice, as to the amount of such provision, but the prudent banker likes to err on the safe side. Probably 2 per cent. of the amount of the banking advances would be a moderate figure to aim at as a minimum for such funds. Besides this, reservation has to be made for rebate of interest on bills current, which is usually taken at a rate to more than cover the currency ; and all other accounting allowances are made on a liberal scale. Shareholders are apt to grumble at too ample reservation of profits ; but it is a policy which pays handsomely in the long run. Indeed, to conduct a bank on any other principle is simply to speculate on the future, and trust to that chapter of accidents which is usually an unfortunate one. The amount of profit thus ascertained constitutes the gross profits. From it there falls to be deducted the expenses of management. The remainder is what is usually styled the net profits.

The total amount of the declared net profits * of the Scottish banks (after adjustment to bring them into uniform shape) was, in 1865, £1,185,813 ; in 1872, £1,244,369 ; in 1883, £1,242,065 ; in 1895, £1,184,988 ; and last year, £1,300,240. † In the two first of these amounts the City of Glasgow Bank return is included, for which, perhaps, some deduction should be made on account of the apocryphal character of that bank's publications.

* See table, chapter i.
† The reports already issued for the current year show a further increase of profits to the extent of £36,000.

But in any case these figures show a surprising amount of steadiness when the magnitude of the sums involved is considered. Too much so, perhaps, for bankers' tastes; but in contrast with the singular unprofitableness of other business in recent years, it is evident that the banker's ability to restrict his outgo as his income slackens is a great standby. When a more detailed examination of years is made, the apparent steadiness is somewhat modified owing to the comparative profitableness of the

APPROPRIATION OF PROFITS. THIRTY-THREE YEARS.

Bank.	Profits.	Applied to			
		Dividend.	Reserve Fund.	Buildings Account.	Sundries.
Bank	£5,402,905	£4,925,000	£257,834	£193,000	£27,071
Royal	6,189,100	5,892,563	205,165	61,682	29,690
British	5,451,561	4,815,000	444,919	160,000	31,642
Commercial	5,134,297	4,560,000	434,297	140,000	—
National	5,327,924	4,775,000	527,195	25,729	—
Union	4,662,765	3,930,000	544,765	155,000	33,000
Clydesdale	4,037,574	3,601,500	309,000	117,000	10,074
Town and County	1,024,175	909,945	65,980	48,250	—
North of Scotland	1,407,643	1,182,640	192,003	22,000	11,000
Caledonian	528,667	427,000	58,268	23,000	20,399
Totals	£39,166,611	£35,018,648	£3,039,426	£945,661	£162,876
Averages, per cent.		89·41	7·76	2·41	0·42
Total Reserved ,,			10·59		

period of "leaps and bounds" in the nation's advancing prosperity. From 1873-8, inclusive, the profits were at high-water mark. There was also an improvement from 1881-3, and again from 1890-3; but in the intervals, and till lately, they have tended towards the old level. The highest point, until last year, was in 1874, when the profits were stated at £1,289,813; and the lowest was in 1868, when they were returned at £1,037,180. The total amount of profits declared by the ten banks during the thirty-two years is £37,780,662.* The under average years were 1865-72 inclusive, 1879-80, 1885-9, and 1894. But in the first specified period there was no actual depression in profits, the reason of the lower range being that the banks had not yet reached the fuller growth to which they subsequently attained. Of the large amount of profit we have stated, $89\frac{1}{2}$ per cent. was absorbed in dividend, and $10\frac{1}{2}$ per cent. was reserved either as addition to the reserve funds proper, or as depreciation of buildings, or otherwise. Thirty years ago, the dividend only amounted to $73\frac{1}{2}$ per cent. of the net profits.

* The profits of the City of Glasgow Bank for fourteen years, and of the Central Bank for one year, falling to be added to show the total amount of profits declared, are £1,523,413. In the appropriation of profits tables in this chapter, the profits declared during the first half of the current year (1897) are included, as also, in some cases, those for 1864. Otherwise, only the years 1865-96, inclusive, are dealt with.

BANK OF SCOTLAND. NET PROFITS.

APPLICATION.

Balance Date.	Amount.	Dividend.		Reserved Funds.		Bank Buildings.	Sundries.
		Rate per Cent.	Amount.	Added.	Withdrawn.		
1863, Dec. 31		9					
1865, Feb. 28	*£161,775	*14	£140,000	£6929		£8000	
1866, ,,	128,658	10½	105,000			5000	
1867, ,,	154,429	†12	120,000	25,000		5000	
1868, ,,	129,721	†12	120,000	25,000		5000	
1869, ,,	132,416	12	120,000			5000	
1870, ,,	123,776	12	120,000				{£17,071 losses
1871, ,,	132,341	12	120,000			5000	
1872, ,,	137,572	12	120,000			5000	
1873, ,,	151,944	12½	125,000	30,000		5000	
1874, ,,	165,221	13½	135,000	25,000		5000	
1875, ,,	175,639	14	140,000	30,000		5000	
1876, ,,	172,234	14	140,000	25,000		5000	
1877, ,,	168,353	14	157,000			5000	{10,000 Centrl. Bk.a/c.
1878, ,,	183,326	14	175,000			5000	
1879, ,,	176,713	13½	168,750			5000	
1880, ,,	168,633	13	162,500			5000	
1881, ,,	176,620	13	162,500			5000	
1882, ,,	177,501	13	162,500	25,000		5000	
1883, ,,	182,549	13½	168,750			10,000	
1884, ,,	187,467	14	175,000			‡10,000	
1885, ,,	177,254	14	175,000			‡5000	
1886, ,,	182,142	14	175,000			‡5000	
1887, ,,	174,266	13½	168,750			‡5000	
1888, ,,	169,204	13	162,500			‡5000	
1889, ,,	162,040	12½	156,250			‡5000	
1890, ,,	165,257	12	150,000	25,000		5000	
1891, ,,	172,102	13	162,500			5000	
1892, ,,	179,828	13	162,500			10,000	
1893, ,,	170.226	13	162,500			5000	
1894, ,,	173,124	13	162,500			5000	
1895, ,,	157,229	12	150 000			5000	
1896, ,,	161,003	12	150,000			10,000	
1897, ,, 27	172,342	12	150,000	25,000 15,905	(Balnce)	‡15,000	
	£5,402,905		£4,925,000 91·15 %	£257,834 4·77 %		£193,000 3·57 %	£27,071 0·51 %

* 14 months, 3 dividends of 4½ per cent., 4½ per cent. and 5 per cent.
† Bonus 1 per cent. included.
‡ £5000 on account of heritable property.

PERIOD OF PUBLISHED ACCOUNTS. 47

BANK OF SCOTLAND REPORTS. ABSTRACT OBSERVATIONS.

Year ending
28th Feb.,
1865. David Davidson, treasurer. Fourteen months' profits; previous balance, 31st Dec., 1863; 10 per cent. bonus to officers.
1867. Unusually profitable; peculiar state of money market.
1870. Loss of £44,000 through Leith forgeries; provided from P. and L. account.
1871. Bank premises account increased by buildings at H. O., Glasgow, and Central Bk. branches;* increased transactions; continued low value of money; no decided revival of trade.
1873. Bank Act, 1844, Amendment Bill: bonus to junior officers.
1876. Great stagnation in manufacturing industry and restricted general business; issue of £375,000 new capital; £250,000 paid up, at 200 per cent.
1877. £375,000 premium on new stock; £340,000 to reserve; £35,000 off Central Bank purchase.
1879. Report of annual meeting; bank's business had progressed; aggravated commercial depression; increased number of failures; succession of bad harvests; heritable property account written down year by year, now below value.
1880. Rate of profit unusually low; long continued stagnation of trade; recent revival of trade; improved money rates; James Adams Wenley appointed treasurer.
1881. Partial recovery of trade; financial retrospect favourable; Bank's Bill.
1883. Larger sum written off property account, °/₁ Edinburgh, New Town office.
1884. Larger sum written off property account, °/₁ exceptional improvements.
1885. Continued depression of industry; absence of commercial demand for money; hint of reduction of interest on deposits; new set of bank notes.
1886. Depression extended to all the great industries; low rates of interest; hint of lowering dividend.
1887. Depression still prevailing, particularly in farming.
1888. Partial improvement; profits moderate.
1889. Contraction of lending in Scotland; centralisation of discounting in London; liberal appropriation necessary to meet bad debts.
1890. Business prosperous; improved demand and prices; higher money rates.
1891. Loan demands well maintained; London rates better; Baring crisis; 16th Feb., robbery of £11,580 of bank notes in London, provided for out of year's profits.
1892. Bank's business well maintained; new London office site purchased.
1893. State of money market and general business not satisfactory.
1894. Bank's business well maintained, especially the advances.
1895. Adverse condition of the money market; bad debts above average.
1896. Ease in the money market; rates low.
1897. Improvement of trade; new London office.

* During last four years.

ROYAL BANK. NET PROFITS.

APPLICATION.

Balance Date.	Amount.	Dividend.		Reserved Funds.		Bank Buildings.	Dundee Bank Purchase Account.
		Rate.	Amount.	Added.	Withdrawn.		
1864, Sep. 24	£185,090	7½	£150,000	£35,090			
1865, ,, 23	177,941	{7½ 3¾}	146,563 75,000		£53,745		
1866, ,, 21	223,742	8	157,333	20,000		£5000	£25,000
1867, ,, 20	179,275	8	157,333	6313		5000	
1868, ,, 18	167,344	8	156,000	20,000			
1869, ,, 17	176,131	8	156,667	20,000		5000	4690
1870, ,, 23	175,624	8	158,667				
1871, ,, 22	170,813	8¼	165,000				
1872, ,, 20	181,432	8½	170,000				
1873, ,, 19	199,328	9	180,000	65,000			
1874, ,, 18	207,178	9¼	190,000			5000	
1875, ,, 17	204,310	9½	190,000			3944	
1876, ,, 22	199,305	9½	190,000			3978	
1877, ,, 21	195,171	9½	190,000			3426	
1878, ,, 20	197,067	9½	190,000	43,454		2039	
1879, Oct. 11	197,189	9½	190,000	6017		1172	
1880, ,, 9	197,693	9½	190,000	4579		3114	
1881, ,, 8	200,291	9½	190,000	9484		807	
1882, ,, 14	210,657	9½	190,000	18,258		2399	
1883, ,, 13	211,735	10	200,000	9574		2160	
1884, ,, 11	196,044	10	200,000		4894	938	
1885, ,, 10	183,992	9	180,000	3746		247	
1886, ,, 9	185,217	9	180,000	4484		732	
1887, ,, 8	185,121	9	180,000	4849		272	
1888, ,, 13	186,950	9	180,000	5032		1918	
1889, ,, 12	188,412	9	180,000	7805		607	
1890, ,, 11	192,077	9	180,000	10,883		1194	
1891, ,, 10	199,753	9	180,000	18,517		1236	
1892, ,, 8	188,682	9	180,000	1781		1901	
1893, ,, 14	188,995	9	180,000	5376		3619	
1894, ,, 13	107,008	8½	170,000		65,486	2489	
1895, ,, 12	164,345	8	160,000	2759		1586	
1896, ,, 10	168,193	8	160,000	6289		1904	
	£6,189,100		£5,892,563	£329,290 124,125	£124,125	£61,682	£29,690
				£205,165			
			95·21 %	3·32 %		0·99 %	0·48 %

PERIOD OF PUBLISHED ACCOUNTS. 49

ROYAL BANK REPORTS.   ABSTRACT OBSERVATIONS.

Year ending
23th Sept.,
1865. Laurence Robertson, cashier.   £45,320 16s. 10d. from suspense account not now required, to rest.
1866. £25,000 written off Dundee Bank purchase account.
1869. £4690, balance of Dundee Bank purchase account written off.
1870. [Dividend paid free of income tax, 2nd half-year and subsequently.]
1871. James Simpson Fleming, cashier.   £30,000 to reserve for dividend equalisation.
1872. Application to Parliament for extension of banking powers.
1873. £100,000 added to rest (including £30,000 as at 1871 above) [15 per cent. bonus on salaries to officers].
1874. London Branch opened (Aug.).
1875. Mercantile and financial embarrassment; opposed Bill to "amend the Bankers Acts".
1876. Continued depression in trade, and difficulty of employing money.
1877. Issue of £180,000 stock held by bank at 220 per cent. (Dec.); sale of Douglas Hotel for £50,000, and the profit (£20,672) written off London property account.
1878. City of Glasgow Bank failure; long period of extreme depression in trade, and three bad harvests had decreased deposits; good harvest, 1878 [5 per cent. bonus to officers].
Oct.,
1879. Proprietors declined to appoint auditors; stagnation in trade; London money rates almost nominal.
1880. Great inactivity of trade, and difficulty in finding permanent investments; bill for extended powers; continued low rates and absence of demand.
1881. Treasury suggestion of a State Legal Tender Note Issue declined; appointment of auditors.
1882. Healthier state of the money market.
1883. Death of William Thomas Thomson, director.   [£5000 presented to cashier.]
1884. Stagnation of trade, and difficulty of employing money.
1885. Changes with regard to rates of interest and discount.
1886. Death of George Mitchell Innes, director.
1890. Baring crisis and guarantee [£300,000 subscribed].
1892. David Robertson Williamson Huie, cashier.
1894. Great increase of difficulty in employing money; exceptionally low rates; considerable losses, chiefly at Dundee.

BRITISH LINEN COMPANY. NET PROFITS.

APPLICATION.

Balance Date.	Amount.	Dividend.		Reserved Funds.		Bank Buildings.	Depreciation of Government Funds.
		Rate Per Cent.	Amount.	Added.	Withdrawn.		
1863, Apr. 15	Balance £2003	11					
1864, ,, 15	118,217	11	£110,000				
1865, ,, 15	151,642	11	110,000			£10,000	£10,000
1866, ,, 14	131,432	11	110,000			5000	21,642
1867, ,, 15	157,270	*13	130,000			5000	
1868, ,, 15	137,138	*13	130,000	£40,840		5000	
1869, ,, 15	139,307	*13	130,000	4307		5000	
1870, ,, 15	136,073	*13	130,000	1073		5000	
1871, ,, 15	137,432	*13	130,000	2432		5000	
1872, ,, 15	143,540	*13	130,000	1349		5000	
1873, ,, 15	134,218	*13	130,000				
1874, ,, 15	163,389	*13	130,000			5000	
1875, ,, 15	160,000	*13	130,000			5000	
1876, ,, 15	150,281	13	130,000			5000	
1877, ,, 14	158,149	14	140,000	13,149		5000	
1878, ,, 15	160,199	14	140,000	20,199			
1879, ,, 15	144,254	13½	135,000	88,259		5000	
1880, ,, 15	145,223	13	130,000			5000	
1881, ,, 15	173,333	13	130,000	50,000		5000	
1882, ,, 15	154,236	14	140,000			5000	
1883, ,, 14	154,418	14	140,000			5000	
1884, ,, 15	153,766	14	140,000			5000	
1885, ,, 15	147,084	14	140,000			5000	
1886, ,, 15	157,874	14	140,000	25,000		5000	
1887, ,, 15	151,287	14	140,000			5000	
1888, ,, 14	152,745	14	140,000	25,000		5000	
1889, ,, 15	158,141	14	140,000			5000	
1890, ,, 15	163,796	14	140,000	25,000		5000	
1891, ,, 15	174,113	14	140,000	25,000		5000	
1892, ,, 15	185,418	14	140,000	50,000		5000	
1893, ,, 15	194,341	15	170,000			5000	
1894, ,, 14	210,177	15	187,500			5000	
1895, ,, 15	202,071	15	187,500			5000	
1896, ,, 15	215,744	16	200,000	32,364		5000	
1897, ,, 15	232,350	18*	225,000	40,947	(Balnce)	5000	
	£5,451,561		£4,815,000	£444,919		£160,000	£31,642
			88·32 %	8·16 %		2·93 %	0·59

* Including bonus.

BRITISH LINEN BANK REPORTS. ABSTRACT OBSERVATIONS.

1865. Patrick Brodie, manager. Government funds written down £10,000.
1866. Recent heavy depreciation of Government securities; balance of last year's profits, £21,642, applied in reduction of cost, bring down to market price.
1867. James Syme, manager [late assistant-manager, Union Bank, Glasgow]. Profits in excess of any previous year, from exceptional causes.
1873. One of the most prosperous years but for losses from failure of Peter Lawson & Son, and defalcations at Newton-Stewart Branch; met by sums set aside for contingencies and from profits of year, without affecting rest.
1875. £15,000 previously written off loss recovered.
1876. £65,000 applied towards allowing full year's dividend to be declared forward; depressed state of trade.
1877. £18,000 recoveries.
1878. 2nd Feb. London Office opened.
1879. Banking disasters; deposits augmented; auditors appointed; dividend arrangement of 1876 reversed. [Printed report of meeting.]
1880. Further additions to deposits; value of money unremunerative; ten additional buildings, ninety-nine offices, sixty-eight property of bank, including H. O., average price £2600; London office removed to 41 Lombard Street. [18th Nov., Circular as to Bills.]
1881. Correspondence with treasury; bills meet with opposition which could only be averted by surrendering right of note issue to be replaced by State Legal Tender Issue; valuable unexhausted powers of which advantage may be taken.
1882. Stock of bank allocated to proprietors, from which, and conversion of an investment, £200,000 added to rest, now increased to £750,000.
1886. Hamilton Andrew Hotson, manager, on Mr. Syme's resignation.
1891. Threatened serious crisis through Barings, guarantee of £300,000.
1892. Issue of £250,000 new stock at 300 per cent., making Capital, £1,250,000, and Reserve Fund, £1,400,000.
1893. Baring guarantee reduced to £75,000.
1896. £67,636 special profits on realisation of securities to Reserve Fund.
1897. £103,407 special profits on realisation of securities to Pension Reserve Fund.

COMMERCIAL BANK. NET PROFITS.

APPLICATION.

Balance Date.	Amount.	Dividend.		Reserved Funds.		Bank Buildings.
		Rate Per Cent.	Amount.	Added.	Withdrawn.	
1864, Oct. 31	£124,906	10	£90,000	£34,906		
1865, ,,	130,913	10½	105,000	20,913		£5000
1866, ,,	155,262	11½	115,000	35,262		5000
1867, ,,	165,511	*14	140,000	20,511		5000
1868, ,,	164,338	14	140,000	19,338		5000
1869, Nov. 1	146,867	14	140,000	4867		5000
1870, Oct. 31	152,168	14	140,000	7168		5000
1871, ,,	153,552	14	140,000	8552		5000
1872, ,,	158,095	14	140,000	13,095		5000
1873, ,,	165,857	15	150,000	10,857		5000
1874, ,,	168,180	15	150,000	13,180		5000
1875, Nov. 1	160,712	15	150,000	5712		5000
1876, Oct. 31	155,538	15	150,000	3538		2000
1877, ,,	157,788	15	150,000	4788		3000
1878, ,,	143,024	13	130,000	11,024		2000
1879, ,,	111,806	12	120,000		£8194	
1880, Nov. 1	151,076	13	130,000	10,837		5000
1881, Oct. 31	146,437	13	130,000	5810		5000
1882, ,,	147,472	14	140,000	10,000		2000
1883, ,,	151,106	14	140,000	5000		3000
1884, ,,	147,530	14	140,000	5000		3000
1885, ,,	148,092	14	140,000			8000
1886, Nov. 1	147,037	14	140,000			5000
1887, Oct. 31	146,024	14	140,000			5000
1888, ,,	151,508	14	140,000			10,000
1889, ,,	158,211	14	140,000	25,000		5000
1890, ,,	168,250	14	140,000	25,000		5000
1891, ,,	175,206	14	140,000	25,000		5000
1892, ,,	165,490	14	140,000	25,000		5000
1893, ,,	181,471	15	150,000	25,000		5000
1894, ,,	165,770	15	150,000			5000
1895, ,,	176,477	15	150,000	25,000		5000
1896, ,,	192,623	16	160,000	25,000		5000
	£5,134,297		£4,560,000	£425,358 8194	£8194	£140,000
				£417,164 17,133	(Blnce)	
				£434,297		
			88·82 %	8·46 %		2·72 %

* Including bonus.

PERIOD OF PUBLISHED ACCOUNTS. 53

COMMERCIAL BANK REPORTS. ABSTRACT OBSERVATIONS.

1864. Alexander Kincaid Mackenzie, manager.
1865. Capital raised from £800,000 to £1,000,000 by transfer from rest; dividend free of tax.
1867. Profits exceptionally large.
1868. [1st Jan. Apology by *Daily Review* for supposition of exceptional means of earning profits.]
1878. City of Glasgow Bank failure; directors not engaged in trade; no foreign or colonial investments; ample yearly provision for bad debts; only one £100,000 advance; losses above average; deposits decreased; diminished trade profits; investment company competition; investments £180,000 above book price.
1879. Great depression in trade and agriculture; losses greater than usual; many failures; bad seasons and low prices; investments £200,000 over book price; bank premises stand in books at £180,128, cost £364,000; heritable property yielding 6¾ per cent. net; and auditors.
1880. Gradual general improvement in business and agriculture.
1881. Sale of £56,000 of bank's own stock at 250 per cent. (Aug.); profit £89,190; registration as limited; 17th Dec., stock converted into shares; improvement in business, but much depression in agriculture.
1882. Robert Luff Peploe, manager; 10th Feb., capital increased to £5,000,000, and limited liability adopted; 3rd April, registration.
1883. Less remunerative rates; losses moderate; July, London Branch opened.
1884. Oct. Andrew Aikman, manager; low value of money; dulness of trade.
1885. Depression prevailing feature in most branches of business and in agriculture; extended powers of investment, India, colonies, and U.S.A. (Govt.).
1886. Continued dulness of trade; depression in agriculture; low value of money.
1887. Higher average value of money.
1888. Greater margin of banking profit, but decreased amount employed; purchase of Lloyds, Barnetts & Bosanquet's office, London.
1890. Guarantee for Baring Brothers & Co.'s obligations.
1891. Result of year's business exceptionally favourable.
1894. Discharge of Baring guarantee (Jan., 1895).
1895. Profit on investments always added to fund for losses; for some years bad debts unimportant; transfer of £100,000 to Reserve Fund, leaving ample sum for contingencies.

NATIONAL BANK. NET PROFITS.

APPLICATION.

Balance Date.	Amount.	Dividend.		Reserved Funds.		Bank Buildings.
		Rate Per Cent.	Amount.	Added.	Withdrawn.	
1864, Nov. 1	£125,023	10	£100,000	£25,023		
1865, ,,	132,140	11	110,000	22,140		
1866, ,,	151,711	*12	120,000	23,211		
1867, ,,	133,610	12	120,000	13,610		
1868, Oct. 31	155,346	*14	140,000	15,346		
1869, Nov. 1	141,495	13	130,000	11,495		
1870, ,,	145,927	13	130,000	8280		
1871, ,,	165,405	*16	160,000	5000		
1872, ,,	158,902	*14½	145,000	7000		£5700
1873, ,,	199,011	*16	160,000	38,000		
1874, Oct. 31	184,645	16	160,000	20,000		
1875, Nov. 1	158,351	*15	150,000	10,000		
1876, ,,	167,699	15	150,000	18,000		
1877, ,,	189,115	15	150,000	42,000		
1878, ,,	158,521	15	150,000			
1879, ,,	131,802	13	130,000			
1880, ,,	155,290	*14	140,000	15,000		
1881, ,,	180,225	*15	150,000	30,000		
1882, ,,	174,897	15	150,000	23,068		
1883, ,,	175,102	*16	160,000	20,000		
1884, ,,	162,152	16	160,000			
1885, Oct. 31	155,082	*15	150,000			
1886, Nov. 1	154,923	15	150,000	10,000		
1887, ,,	152,788	15	150,000			
1888, ,,	156,031	15	150,000	10,000		
1889, ,,	171,116	15	150,000	20,000		
1890, ,,	176,594	15	150,000	25,000		
1891, Oct. 31	173,394	15	150,000	25,000		
1892, Nov. 1	161,322	15	150,000	10,000		
1893, ,,	171,142	15	150,000	25,000		
1894, ,,	156,828	15	150,000			
1895, ,,	159,041	15	150,000	5000		
1896, ,,	198,344	*16	160,000	30,000		20,029
	£5,327,924		£4,775,000	£507,173		£25,729
				20,022	(Balnce)	
				£527,195		
			89·62 %	9·90 %		0·48 %

* Including bonus.

NATIONAL BANK REPORTS. ABSTRACT OBSERVATIONS.

1864. William James Duncan, manager. London Branch open.
1865. Dividend and bonus free of income tax.
1866. Sums laid aside for depreciation of heritable property and the public funds; £8500 laid aside for unforeseen contingencies.
1867. Sums laid aside for depreciation of heritable property and the public funds; the £8500 last year had not been required and was again carried forward.
1868. Incidental profits enabling bonus of 2 per cent.; the £8500 again carried forward.
1869. The £8500 again carried forward.
1870. £5110 written off heritable property.
1871. Depreciation of property provided for; sundry incidental profits.
1872. No casual sources of income.
1873. Sundry incidental profits; large increase of bank's business last two or three years; depreciation of property provided for.
1874. Depreciation of property provided for.
1875. Depreciation of property provided for; rate of earning lower than usual.
1876. Depreciation of property provided for; long continued low rate of interest; bad debts above average.
1877. Depreciation of property provided for; low value of money; losses unusually small; variety of casual profits; £30,000 transferred from provision for losses to rest.
1878. Singularly even flow of business; steady moderate rate of profit; singularly moderate amount of losses; large number of failures; losses indirectly from City Bank failure, not exceed £5000; properties stand in books at sum far within estimated value; very ample guarantee fund against risks of loss; London and Glasgow offices entirely satisfactory; Government securities stand at low prices; steady application of sound principles of business.
1879. Results not so favourable as usual; unusually low value of money, and further difficulty of employing money; large accession of business; unfavourable state of mercantile and agricultural pursuits; losses above average; business sound and satisfactory.
1880. Very moderate rate of profits; losses very moderate; letters and articles in newspapers about limited liability.
1881. Thomas Hector Smith, manager. Rate of profit very moderate; incidental profits; losses unusually small; very ample provision for safety. Mr. Duncan's retirement.
1882. Registration as limited (3rd Apr.); good demand for money at fair rates; sale of £41,918 10s. of bank's own stock, realising profit of £71,932 7s. 11d.
1883. Satisfactory results.
1884. Low value of money; unsatisfactory state of business.
1885. General depression of trade; difficulty of fully employing funds.
1886. Circumstances similar to last year.
1889. Improvement in business generally.
1890. Baring crisis and guarantee referred to.
1891. Business in every way satisfactory.
1892. Condition of money market unfavourable.
1894. Very restricted demand for advances; abnormally low rates.
1895. Circumstances similar to those of 1894, unfavourable.
1896. Satisfactory results of the past year's business.

UNION BANK. NET PROFITS.

Balance Date.			Amount.	Dividend.		Reserved Funds.		Bank Bldngs.	Collie Losses.
				Rate Per Cent.	Amount.	Added.	Withdrawn.		
1864.	Apr.	2	£118,168	8	£80,000	£38,168			
1865,	,,	1	148,028	8	80,000	63,028		£5000	
1866,	,,	2	136,304	9	90,000	41,304		5000	
1867,	,,	2	163,619	10	100,000	36,300		5000	
1868,	,,	2	121,788	10	100,000	20,000		5000	
1869,	,,	2	129,068	11	110,000	20,000		5000	
1870,	,,	2	135,633	12	120,000	10,000		5000	
1871,	,,	1	132,363	12	120,000	7000		5000	
1872,	,,	2	140,356	13	130,000	5000		5000	
1873,	,,	2	160,597	15	150,000			10,000	
1874.	,,	2	162,583	15	150,000	6000		5000	
1875,	,,	2	161,494	15	150,000	7000		5000	
1876,	,,	1	156,809	13	130,000				£33,000
1877,	,,	2	145,024	13	130,000	15,000			
1878,	,,	2	146,446	13	130,000	15,000			
1879,	,,	2	131,434	12	120,000			5000	
1880,	,,	2	127,553	12	120,000			5000	
1881,	,,	2	133,172	12	120,000	10,000		5000	
1882,	,,	1	133,165	12	120,000	10,000		5000	
1883,	,,	2	145,793	12	120,000	20,000		5000	
1884,	,,	2	137,662	12	120,000	10,000		5000	
1885,	,,	2	117,095	12	120,000				
1886,	,,	2	127,102	12	120,000			5000	
1887,	,,	2	125,060	12	120,000			5000	
1888,	,,	2	132,980	11	110,000	20,000		5000	
1889,	,,	2	134,486	11	110,000	20,000		5000	
1890,	,,	2	133,354	11	110,000	20,000		5000	
1891,	,,	2	129,604	11	110,000	10,000		5000	
1892,	,,	2	131,007	11	110,000	20,000		5000	
1893,	,,	2	131,644	11	110,000	15,000		5000	
1894,	,,	2	135,049	11	110,000	20,000		5000	
1895,	,,	2	115,940	10	100,000	10,000		5000	
1896,	,,	2	137,215	10	100,000	25,000		10,00	
1897,	,,	2	145,675	11	110,000	25,000 25,965	(Balnce)	5000	
			£4,662,765		£3,930,000 84·50 %	£544,765 11·44 %		£155,000 3·33 %	£33,000 0·73 %

UNION BANK REPORTS. ABSTRACT OBSERVATIONS.

1864. James Robertson and Charles Gairdner, joint managers (1862). Perth Bank purchase account gradually reduced since 1857, balance, £36,956 7s., now written off entirely; £30,000 brought from guarantee fund to P. and L.
1865. Charles Gairdner, manager; Mr. Robertson's retirement. Another prosperous year.
1867. Death of Sir John Stuart Forbes, Bart., Chairman; and Sir Adam Hay, Bart., for fifty years partner of Forbes & Co., and director of bank.
1868. Alterations of bank's contract.
1869. Number of directors fixed at ten [a reduction].
1873. Recoveries from old outstanding accounts (which, in 1862, occasioned anxiety, and transfer of large sum from rest), and other receipts, £62,447 8s. 7d.; £62,000 restored to rest.
1874. Bad debts exceptionally large; death of Adam Black, director.
1875. Alteration of contract.
1876. Heavy loss by failures in London; false and fraudulent representations in reference to securities; warrant for apprehension of Alexander Collie, evaded by flight; £120,000 transferred to strengthen fund for provision for losses; £87,000 from rest, and £33,000 from P. and L.
1877. Great depression in trade; money rates unusually low.
1878. 28th March. London Branch opened; chief officer to be styled general manager.
1879. Banking and commercial disasters; bank but little affected; new head offices; bank owns seventy-nine branch offices; auditors appointed.
1880. Margin of profit unusually low.
1881. Limited liability question making progress towards solution.
1882. 3rd April. Registered as limited; dividend warrants to be sent by post.
1885. Low margin of profit; continued depression in trade.
1886. Diminishing demand for money, as in preceding year; slight alteration in contract of co-partnery.
1887. More hopeful feeling regarding trade.
1888. Marquess of Bute elected chairman.
1889. Death of Dr. Anderson Kirkwood, director.
1891. Baring difficulties, and guarantee of £300,000; death of Mr. A. B. M'Grigor.
1895. Robert Blyth, general manager. Depression in trade; more than usual difficulty in remunerative employment of money; Baring guarantee extinguished without loss; Dr. Gairdner's resignation.
1896. Death of Sir John Adam Hay, Bart., director.

CLYDESDALE BANK. NET PROFITS.

Balance Date.	Amount.	Dividend.		Reserved Funds.		Bank Buildings.	Depreciation of Consols.
		Rate Per Cent.	Amount.	Added.	Withdrawn.		
1864, June 14	£9508	9					
1865, ,,	112,151	*4½	£40,500	£15,000		£5000	
1865, Dec. 31	56,073	10	90,000	15,000		3000	
1866, ,,	122,553	10	90,000	10,000		7000	£10,074
1867, ,,	95,254	10	90,000			5000	
1868, ,,	102,968	†11	99,000	8000		2000	
1869, ,,	113,015	11	99,000	7000		3000	
1870, ,,	119,969	‡12	108,000	5000		§10,000	
1871, ,,	117,804	12	108,000	10,000			
1872, ,,	137,421	13	117,000			5000	
1873, ,,	153,740	14	140,000	19,663			
1874, ,,	144,914	14	140,000			5000	
1875, ,,	129,114	14	140,000				
1876, ,,	137,667	14	140,000				
1877, ,,	140,419	14	140,000				
1878, ,,	120,635	12	120,000				
1879, ,,	106,690	11	110,000				
1880, ,,	126,597	12	120,000				
1881, ,,	133,934	12	120,000	10,000		5000	
1882, ,,	148,312	13	130,000	8694			
1883, ,,	125,472	12	120,000			6000	
1884, ,,	114,458	12	120,000				
1885, ,,	126,884	12	120,000			5000	
1886, ,,	121,798	10	100,000	27,329			
1887, ,,	112,800	10	100,000	7000		3000	
1888, ,,	107,851	10	100,000	5000		3000	
1889, ,,	119,261	10	100,000	10,000		7500	
1890, ,,	130,143	10	100,000	25,000		5000	
1891, ,,	131,733	10	100,000	25,000		5000	
1892, ,,	125,688	10	100,000	20,000		5000	
1893, ,,	130,025	10	100,000	25,000		5000	
1894, ,,	114,439	10	100,000			10,000	
1895, ,,	121,249	10	100,000	19,665		5000	
1896, ,,	132,035	10	100,000	25,000		7500	
	£4,037,574		£3,601,500	£297,351 11,649 (Balnce)		£117,000	£10,074
			89·19 %	£309,000 7·65 %		2·90 %	0·25 %

* Half-year.   † Not ex. income tax.   ‡ Including bonus.   § º/a site for new H. O.

PERIOD OF PUBLISHED ACCOUNTS. 59

CLYDESDALE BANK REPORTS. ABSTRACT OBSERVATIONS.

1864. George Readman, manager.
1865. Period (to June) one of more than usual anxiety in banking affairs; great fluctuation in value of money, goods, and produce; mercantile failures; banking profits very satisfactory; alteration of balance to 31st Dec.
1866. Profits exceptional; dividend free of income tax.
1867. Reduced value of money; general contraction of business; difficulty of finding employment for capital.
1868. Value of money unusually low.
1869. Some improvement in value and demand for money; trade of Glasgow sound.
1870. Site of new Head Office acquired.
1871. Recovery of £10,074 of previous depreciation in securities now realised, of which £10,000 carried to Reserve Fund in addition to £10,000 from P. and L.
1872. High value of money; unusual freedom from bad debts.
1873. Profits most satisfactory; £30,000 from recoveries and premium realised; £100,000 new stock issued to proprietors at 240 per cent. with accrued dividend (2nd March); branches to be opened in Cumberland, at Carlisle, Workington, and Whitehaven.
1874. New H. O. opened; value of money under average; bad debts more than usual; Miller Street premises sold at profit of £25,000, distributed as bonus of 2½ per cent.; Superannuation Fund proposed; £200,000 added to Reserve Fund.
1875. Numerous mercantile failures; £15,000 special provision for bad debts.
1876. Dulness of trade; very low price of money.
1877. 1st Dec. London Branch opened; retiring directors to be ineligible for one year.
1878. Bad debts considerably in excess of average; chief officer to be designated general manager; advances of every kind in a satisfactory state; every bad debt written off, and ample provision made for doubtful cases; freehold premises bought in London.
1879. Unfavourable for banking; trade much depressed; bad debts incurred; large unemployed funds; advances in a sound state; auditors appointed; only one retiring director to be disqualified. [Annual Meeting, proceedings printed.]
1880. John Maxwell Cunningham, general manager. Improvement in business of country, but value of money low; fair demand for capital; adoption of limited liability engaging attention. Mr. Readman's resignation.
1881. Improvement in trade; agricultural depression; rates for money low till Oct.; adoption of limited liability; conversion of stock into shares; and alteration of contract proposed.
1882. Profit of £41,305 15s. on sale of own shares carried to Reserve Fund; 3rd Apr., registered as The Clydesdale Bank, Limited; dividend warrants to be sent by post.
1883. Bad debts exceeded average; shortening transfer closing period.
1885. Depression of agricultural, commercial, and manufacturing interests, but business of bank well maintained and resources fully employed.
1886. George Readman, managing director. Heavy exceptional losses from extreme depression in produce, and on other accounts; £132,000 transferred from Reserve Fund to a suspense account, and £27,329 from year's profits. Mr. Cunningham's resignation.
1887. George Readman, managing director; David Wilson, general manager. Last year's transfers to suspense found sufficient; business satisfactory; directors to be not fewer than seven or more than nine.
1888. David Wilson, general manager. Reserve Fund now £440,000.
1889. Extension of sphere from which directors may be chosen.
1890. Baring guarantee; alterations of contract carried out.
1891. Reserve Fund now £500,000.
1894. Exceptional losses, £114,665 at Dundee, written off Reserve Fund; Baring guarantee cancelled 11th Feb., 1895; purchase of more freehold property in London.

TOWN AND COUNTY BANK. NET PROFITS.

APPLICATION.

Balance Date.	Amount.	Dividend.		Reserved Funds.		Bank Buildings.
		Rate Per Cent.	Amount.	Added.	Withdrawn.	
1864, Jan. 31	Bal., £435	10				
1865, ,,	30,529	10	£15,600	£14,000		£1250
1866, ,,	27,937	10	15,600	11,000		1250
1867, ,,	31,024	10	18,200	10,000		1250
1868, ,,	27,913	10	18,200	10,000		1250
1869, ,,	19,825	10	18,200			1250
1870, ,,	19,583	10	18,200			1500
1871, ,,	21,408	10	18,200	2000		1500
1872, ,,	23,138	10	18,200	3000		1500
1873, ,,	22,714	11¼	20,475			1500
1874, ,,	32,923	12½	31,500			1500
1875, ,,	33,777	12½	31,500			1500
1876, ,,	36,982	13¾	34,650			1500
1877, ,,	36,277	13¾	34,650			1500
1878, ,,	36,286	13¾	34,650			1500
1879, ,,	32,387	12½	31,500			1500
1880, ,,	31,709	12½	31,500			1500
1881, ,,	32,826	12½	31,500			1500
1882, ,,	33,068	12½	31,500			1500
1883, ,,	32,650	12½	31,500			1500
1884, ,,	30,470	11½	28,980			1500
1885, ,,	30,748	11½	28,980			1500
1886, ,,	31,066	11½	28,980			1500
1887, ,,	31,368	11¾	29,610			1500
1888, ,,	31,412	11¾	29,610			1500
1889, ,,	32,437	12	30,240			1500
1890, ,,	32,566	12	30,240			1500
1891, ,,	32,884	12	30,240			1500
1892, ,,	32,949	12	30,240	4000		1500
1893, ,,	34,461	12½	31,500			1500
1894, ,,	34,646	12½	31,500	4000		1500
1895, ,,	34,372	12½	31,500			1500
1896, ,,	35,906	12½	31,500	4000		1500
1897, ,,	35,439	12½	31,500	3980	(Bal.)	1500
	£1,024,175		£909,945	£65,980		£48,250
			88·85 %	6·43 %		4·72 %

PERIOD OF PUBLISHED ACCOUNTS. 61

Town and County Bank Reports. Abstract Observations.

1865. William Littlejohn, manager and cashier. Exceptional state of money market (to 31st Jan.).
1866. Altered condition of money market; £26,000 transferred from guarantee fund to capital and bonus of £1 per share. In 1862 a similar transference was made.
1867. Satisfactory condition of money market, and increasing business.
1868. Unusually low rates for money.
1870. £25,000 written off guarantee fund to meet depression of market value of some investments and securities.
1872. £15,000 restored to guarantee fund by improvement in value of investments and securities.
1873. 10,000 new shares issued (12th June, 1872) at £7 premium; £70,000 carried to guarantee fund; two sub-offices to be opened in Aberdeen—Western and Northern.
1874. £3150 casual profits; harbour branch, Aberdeen, opened; also branches in Dundee, Perth and Fochabers.
1875. Bank in sound and prosperous condition; Superannuation Fund established to mark fiftieth anniversary.
1876. 500 guineas (including piece plate) presented to manager; George Livingston Rorie, assistant manager (1st Dec., 1875).
1877. £10,000 restored to guarantee fund from profits on investments realised, etc., and £1000 added also from casual profits.
1878. George Livingston Rorie, manager and cashier, 31st January; Mr. Littlejohn retiring. Proposal to issue more shares delayed.
1879. Bank buildings written down 33½ per cent. of original cost; expectation of Government measure on joint stock banks; expiry of contract, 5th March, 1880; proposed prorogation for twenty-one years; all bad and doubtful debts amply provided for, and assurance of soundness.
1880. Long continued depression in trade; bad harvests; low rates; scarcity of investments; limited liability question; prorogation of contract till 1901.
1881. Limited liability still under consideration.
1882. No material increase in demand for money; to be registered as limited on 3rd April.
1884. John Findlater, manager and cashier. Profits and losses both over average; depression of trade and agriculture; advances sound and healthy.
1885. Continued depression in agricultural and commercial affairs.
1886. Losses heavier than ordinary; continued depression in agricultural and commercial affairs.
1887. Fairly remunerative employment for funds; low prices of cereals and live stock.
1888. Profits satisfactory; last three years' losses chiefly by failures in herring-curing trade; ample provision made; less demand for money.
1889. Business satisfactory, but deposit receipt rate too high.
1890. No special remarks.
1891. Death of Mr. Findlater, manager.
1892. Thomas Cochrane, manager and cashier.

North of Scotland Bank. Net Profits.

Balance Date.	Amount.	Dividend.		Reserved Funds.		Bank Buildings.	Depreciation of Consols.
		Rate Per Cent.	Amount.	Added.	Withdrawn.		
1864, Sep. 30	{ Balance £1295	10					£3500
1865, ,,	38,475	10	£28,000	£10,000			
1866, ,,	41,527	10	28,000	10,000			
1867, ,,	38,004	10	28,000	10,000			
1868, ,,	33,495	10	28,000	5000			
1869, ,,	34,209	10	32,000	2500			
1870, ,,	34,580	10	32,000	2500			
1871, ,,	37,135	10	32,000	5000			
1872, ,,	37,654	10	32,000	6000			
1873, ,,	40,186	10	32,000	10,000			
1874, ,,	45,236	*11¼	36,000	9000			
1875, ,,	50,291	12½	46,294			£2000	
1876, ,,	52,309	12½	49,108			1000	
1877, ,,	55,192	*13¾	54,145			1000	
1878, ,,	54,066	12½	49,312			1000	
1879, ,,	52,233	12½	49,313	8000			
1880, ,,	51,569	12½	49,312				
1881, ,,	51,800	12½	49,656	466		2000	
1882, ,,	50,661	12½	50,000				
1883, ,,	49,936	12½	50,000			1000	
1884, ,,	52,504	12½	50,000			2000	
1885, ,,	52,848	12½	50,000			2500	
1886, ,,	54,863	12½	50,000	5000		2500	
1887, ,,	50,938	12½	50,000			1000	
1888, ,,	41,045	6¼	25,000	15,000			
1889, ,,	36,131	6¼	25,000	10,000			
1890, ,,	36,176	6¼	25,000	7500			7500
1891, ,,	36,596	6¼	25,000	10,000		1000	
1892, ,,	37,086	6¼	25,000	10,000		1000	
1893, ,,	37,388	6¼	25,000	12,500		†1000	
1894, ,,	38,714	6¼	25,000	12,500		†1000	
1895, ,,	40,110	6¼	25,000	12,500		†1000	
1896, ,,	43,396	6·875	27,500	17,500		†1000	
	£1,407,643		£1,182,640	£1037	(Balnce)	£22,000	£11,000
				£192,003			
			84·02 %	13·64 %		1·56 %	0·78 %

* Including bonus.   † Heritable Property Account.

NORTH OF SCOTLAND BANK REPORTS. ABSTRACT OBSERVATIONS.

1864. Death of Mr. Westland, manager.
1865. Jan. Robert Lumsden, manager. Rates of interest less remunerative; some losses of an exceptional character.
1866. Continued depression of consols; £3500 applied to reduce cost.
1867. Low rates of interest; business of bank prosperous.
1868. Low rates of interest; £15,000 applied to reduce investments to market value; £40,000, or 10s. per share, added to capital from Reserve Fund.
1869. Slight improvement in return for money.
1870. Great rise in value of money in July; proposed reduction of directors from eleven to seven objected to by board; sub-office in Aberdeen opened.
1871. Qualification of directors increased from fifty to 100 shares.
1872. Business satisfactory; £9000 replaced to Reserve Fund from favourable realisation of stocks.
1873. Town branches in Aberdeen.
1874. Prosperous business; bonus of 25s. per cent.; issue of 9706 new shares at £9 to shareholders; £6000 restored to Reserve Fund.
1875. Desire to reduce Property Account greatly below actual value; issue of 7338 shares at £10; premiums received, £92,558.
1876. Issue of 364 shares at £6, and 992 at £7 premium; depression of trade; premium, £9128. Profits narrow, business contracted.
1877. £3209 12s. recoveries applied to form nucleus of Officials' Benefit Fund; £1440 premiums on new shares.
1878. Above fund made a mutual guarantee fund, bank giving five yearly sums of £250; City of Glasgow Bank; general depression in agriculture and trade; excellent harvest.
1879. Depression of trade; Banking and Joint Stock Companies Bill; audit; £8000 written off for contingencies.
1880. Edward Fiddes, joint manager. Slight recovery from long depression of trade, but rates of interest low.
1881. Issue of 1375 new shares, at £9092 11s. 3d. premium; limited liability desired.
1882. Registration as limited; agricultural depression passing away.
1883. Rates of interest more remunerative.
1884. Increased trade demand for money.
1885. Depression in trade and agriculture.
1886. Depreciation and unsaleableness of landed property; £18,000 written off certain advances from Reserve Fund.
1887. Fishcuring trade crisis; £100,000 written off Reserve Fund.
1888. Edward Fiddes, manager. £100,000 (balance) written off Reserve Fund, and £15,000 from year's profits.
1889. George Anderson, manager. Adverse rates of interest, and lower investment returns; death of Mr. Fiddes.
1890. Large increase in business; sharp fall in prices of investment stocks; £7500 applied in reduction of prices.
1891. Business of bank has prospered.
1896. £7500 from exceptional profits added to Reserve Fund.

CALEDONIAN BANK. NET PROFITS.

APPLICATION.

Balance Date.	Amount.	Dividend.		Reserved Funds.		Bank Bldings.	Depreciation.
		Rate Per Cent.	Amount.	Added.	Withdrawn.		
1864, June 30	Balance £766	9					
1865, ,,	23,186	10	£12,500	£9000		£750	
1866, ,,	16,076	10	12,500	4000		750	
1867, ,,	18,342	10	12,500	4000		750	
1868, ,,	17,134	10	12,500	4000		750	
1869, ,,	17,009	11	13,750	2000		1000	
1870, ,,	17,288	12	15,000			1000	
1871, ,,	18,070	12	15,000	2000		1000	
1872, ,,	24,499	*14	17,500	8500		1000	
1873, ,,	18,717	14	17,500			1000	
1874, ,,	18,694	14	17,500			1000	
1875, ,,	20,831	14	17,500			1000	
1876, ,,	24,186	14	21,000			5500	
1877, ,,	24,117	14	21,000				
1878, ,,	22,682	14	21,000				
1879, ,,	10,552	nil.					£16,399
1880, ,,	5507	3	4500				
1881, ,,	9785	6½	9750				
1882, ,,	12,553	7	10,500	2000			
1883, ,,	13,244	7½	11,250	1000			1000
1884, ,,	13,784	7½	11,250	2000			
1885, ,,	13,023	7½	11,250	1000		500	
1886, ,,	13,143	7½	11,250	1000		500	
1887, ,,	12,436	7½	11,250	1000		500	
1888, ,,	11,211	7½	11,250				
1889, ,,	12,467	8	12,000	1000			
1890, ,,	14,476	8	12,000	1000		500	
1891, ,,	14,172	8	12,000	2000		500	
1892, ,,	16,970	8	12,000	2000		1000	2000
1893, ,,	16,494	8	12,000	2000		500	2000
1894, ,,	15,832	8	12,000	3000		1000	
1895, ,,	14,154	8	12,000	1000		1000	
1896, ,,	14,781	8	12,000	1000		1000	
1897, ,,	13,486	8	12,000	1000		500	
				2768	(Blnce)		
	£528,667		£427,000	£58,268		£23,000	£20,399
			80·77 %	11·02 %		4·35 %	3·86 %

* Including bonus.

CALEDONIAN BANK REPORTS.   ABSTRACT OBSERVATIONS.

1865. Charles Waterston, manager. More profitable character of business during first half-year (1864); premiums on securities realised.
1866. Four West Coast Branches opened.
1867. Branch at Burghead opened; £1000 presented to manager.
1868. Dividend to be payable half-yearly in future.
1869. Increase of Guarantee Fund, restricted to 4 per cent. interest thereon.
1872. Profit on sale of old investments.
1873. Bonus of 10 per cent. on salaries.
1874. 10,000 new shares (£2 10s. called up) to be allotted 1st Jan., 1875, at £3 15s., 2000 to be sold [never carried out].
1875. £12,500 premium on 10,000 new shares placed to Reserve Fund.
1876. 50 per cent. having been written off House Property Account, special appropriation to be discontinued.
1877. Appropriation to bank's premises new account.
1878. Appropriation to bank's premises new account; Mr. Waterston's retirement.
1879. Dec., 1878, suspension of business; £75,892 13s. 2d. placed to Suspense Account, including £25,000 from Reserve Fund; Aug., 1879, resumed business.
1880. Eagle Henderson Macmillan, manager (2nd Feb.). Six months' operations.
1881. Unprecedented severity of winter; depression of trade; adoption of limited liability.
1882. 3rd Apr. Registered as limited; directors to be reduced from nine to seven.
1893. William MacGregor, accountant, proposed as director.

CITY OF GLASGOW BANK. NET PROFITS.

Balance Date.	Amount.	Dividend.		Reserved Funds.		Bank Bldngs.	Bank of Mona Defalcations.
		Rate Per Cent.	Amount.	Added.	Withdrawn.		
1859, June	£35,259	3	£20,126	£15,133			
1860, ,,	41,115	4	26,835	10,000			
1861, ,,	43,406	5	33,543	10,000			
1862, ,,	45,218	5	33,543	14,867			
1863, ,,	46,400	5	33,544	10,000			
1864, ,,	66,562	6	46,226	15,261			
1865, ,, 7	89,646	7	60,900	25,000		£5000	
1866, ,,	92,494	7	60,900	20,000			
1867, ,,	102,288	8	69,600	20,000		5000	
1868, ,,	93,206	8	69,600	20,000		10,000	
1869, ,,	97,776	8	69,600	30,000		5000	
1870, ,,	92,752	9	78,300	10,000		5000	
1871, ,,	96,483	9	78,300	10,000		5000	
1872, ,,	101,760	10	87,000	10,000		5000	
1873, ,,	113,284	10	87,000	20,000		10,000	
1874, ,, 3	128,712	11	110,000	11,500		5000	
1875, ,, 2	126,019	11	110,000	15,000		5000	
1876, ,, 7	124,388	11	110,000			5000	
1877, ,, 6	127,011	12	120,000			10,000	
1878, ,, 5	125,094	12	120,000				£8873
	£1,788,874		£1,425,017	£13,223	(Balnce)	£75,000	£8873
				£279,984			
			79·66 %	15·65 %		4·19 %	0·50 %

CITY OF GLASGOW BANK REPORTS. ABSTRACT OBSERVATIONS.

1858. Robert Salmond, manager. £71,588 5s. 4d., due to Capital Account, carried to Contingent Fund to be reduced by yearly instalments of £20,000 out of profits. [Proposal found to be illegal and loss written off.]
1859. Improvement in position and prospects of bank; recent stoppage; reduction of capital by £74,541. "With regard to the future management of the bank, safety and economy are the two objects which the directors desire especially to keep in view." Number of branches withdrawn.
1862. Increasing prosperity; extreme depression of trade, and low rates of interest; re-establishment of Edinburgh Board; Earl of Caithness elected governor, and Sir William Dunbar, deputy governor; dividend free of income tax.
1863. Depression in rural and manufacturing districts; rates of interest low; 29th Nov., registered under Companies Act.
1864. Alexander Stronach, manager. Business highly satisfactory; £99,131 new stock issued at £59,739 6s. premium.
1865. Business highly prosperous, future prospects encouraging, etc.
1867. New Edinburgh office.
1869. General depression of trade; low rates; business satisfactory; prospects encouraging; policy of board to establish a strong Reserve Fund.
1870. Progress steady and satisfactory; proposed increase of capital.
1871. Low rates; progress perfectly satisfactory.
1874. £130,000 new stock issued; premium (seemingly) £143,500 to Reserve Fund.
1876. Robert Summers Stronach, manager. Alexander Stronach, retiring. Enlargement of H. O. premises indispensable.
1877. Plans of H. O. extension.
1878. June. Defalcation at Bank of Mona, £8873 off year's profits. New premises progressing.
1878. 2nd Oct. Failed; estimated losses, £6,640,983.

Individually the banks have had varied experience, and have manifested diversity of policy. The profits of the Bank of Scotland have varied considerably, from £123,776 in 1870 to £187,467 in 1884. The dividend, which has never exceeded the sum of the year's profits, has ranged from $9\frac{1}{2}$ per cent. to 14 per cent., and is now at 12 per cent. In all, the dividend has absorbed 91 per cent. of the total profits, 9 per cent. having been reserved. The Royal Bank shows larger aggregate profits than any of the other banks; its dividend rose from $7\frac{1}{2}$ per cent. to 10 per cent., and is now 8 per cent.; it has divided $95\frac{1}{4}$ per cent. and reserved $4\frac{3}{4}$ per cent. of net profits. The British Linen Company's dividend has fluctuated very little. It has risen from 11 per cent. to 16 per cent., at which it now stands, and has never exceeded the year's profits. For the year to 15th April last a bonus or extra dividend of 2 per cent. has been declared. The dividend has absorbed 88 per cent. of the profits, 12 per cent. having been reserved. The Commercial Bank's dividend (including bonuses) has varied from 10 per cent. to 16 per cent., at which it now stands; 89 per cent. of profits have been divided, and 11 per cent. reserved. The net profits were only once exceeded by the dividend. The National Bank's dividend and bonus have fluctuated from 10 per cent. to 16 per cent., the present rate. The proprietors have taken $89\frac{1}{2}$ per cent., and reserved $10\frac{1}{2}$ per cent., and have never exceeded the year's profits. The Union Bank's dividend has varied from 8 per cent. to 15 per cent., and now stands at 11 per cent., and has absorbed $84\frac{1}{2}$ per cent. of the profits, $15\frac{1}{2}$ per cent. being reserved. The Clydesdale Bank dividend has varied from 10 per cent. to 14 per cent., and now stands at 10 per cent.; 89 per cent. have been distributed, and 11 per cent. reserved. The Town and County Bank's dividend rose from 10 per cent. to 13¾ per cent., and is now 12½ per cent.; 89 per cent. have been distributed, and 11 per cent. reserved. The North of Scotland Bank's dividend rose from 10 per cent. to 13¾ per cent., and is now about 6¾ per cent.; 84 per cent. have been distributed and 16 per cent. reserved. The Caledonian Bank's dividend rose from 10 per cent. to 14 per cent. previous to the trials of 1878-79, and has since gradually risen to 8 per cent.; 80½ per cent. of profits have been paid in dividend and 19½ per cent. have been reserved. None of the provincial banks has ever paid in dividend more than the year's net profits. The following table gives fuller details, in connection with which it may be interesting to mention that the City of Glasgow Bank statements represent it to have divided 79½ per cent. and reserved 20½ per cent.:—

APPROPRIATION OF THIRTY-THREE YEARS' PROFITS.

Name.	To Dividend.	To Reserve.	To Buildings.	To Depreciation.
	Per Cent.	Per Cent.	Per Cent.	Per Cent.
Bank - - - - -	91¼	4¾	3½	½
Royal - - - -	95¼	3¼	1	½
British - - - -	88¼	8¼	3	½
Commercial - -	88¾	8½	2¾	—
National - - - -	89½	10	0½	—
Union - - - -	84½	11½	3¼	¾
Clydesdale - - -	89	7¾	3	¼
Town and County -	88¾	6½	4¾	—
North of Scotland	84	13¾	1½	¾
Caledonian - - -	80¾	11	4¼	4

It is a noticeable feature that a much smaller proportion of profits has been reserved during the later than during the earlier years of the period. The growing difficulty in making profits, conjoined with a natural reluctance to reduce dividends when they were actually earned, has probably influenced this result; but no doubt the large additions made to reserves from incidental income (such as premiums on new stock) have superinduced a feeling that the business profits might be somewhat relieved from the burden for a time. It does not appear, however, that the British Linen Company, the Commercial Bank, or the Union Bank should be included in this category. The Clydesdale and North of Scotland Banks have also made large transfers from business profits in recent years; but, with the exception of handsome sums applied yearly to write down the cost of buildings, these were required to replace losses.

In most cases the net profits for 1895 showed an improvement over those for 1865, the exceptions being the Royal, Union, and Caledonian Banks, but in only two or three was the increase of a substantial character. The British Linen Company and Commercial Bank increased their profits by 33 per cent. and 35 per cent. respectively, and the National Bank by 20 per cent. The Bank of Scotland and Town and County Bank followed with 13 per cent. The other banks either showed but trifling improvements or a falling off; the most striking instance of the latter experience being the Union Bank, whose profits were actually £32,088, or 22 per cent., less. The average experience gave an improvement of nearly 10 per cent. over the ten banks. The average dividend, however, rose at a greater ratio, being more than 2 per cent. higher than in 1865. In other words, while formerly dividend absorbed $73\frac{1}{2}$ per cent. of the profits, the proprietors, thirty years later, were taking 90 per cent. In 1896, however, a decided change took place. The declared profits showed a marked upward movement, which was most noticeable in the cases of the National, Commercial, and British Linen. It was accompanied by an increase of dividends by these banks, by which the general average has been raised to 11 4·5 per cent. This improvement can hardly be attributed to increased earnings. No doubt business was better, but not to an extent sufficient to raise the net receipts by $9\tfrac{3}{4}$ per cent. on the year's turnover. It is pretty evident that the banks (or some of them) are showing their hands more freely. Among the reports issued during the current year is that of the British Linen Company, which again breaks the record. In declaring net profits for the year amounting to £232,350, it not only far exceeds all its own previous reports, but also those of all the other banks. The nearest approach to that declaration was by the Royal Bank in 1866, with £223,742 of profits. This favourable experience has provided a bonus of 2 per cent. to the proprietors, making the total dividend 18 per cent. for the year, the highest rate ever paid by any Scottish bank in modern times.

In considering the relationship of branch extension to realisation of profit, a very diverse experience is seen. All the banks have extended their branch systems, but they have done so in varying degrees and with different results. The Bank of Scotland and the provincial banks, occupying throughout the period much the same positions relatively to the other banks as regards number of branches, have not materially changed their relative places in regard to amount of profits, although the former has gone back slightly. The Royal Bank, which has largely increased its branch system, shows a decrease in profits; while the British Linen Company and the Commercial Bank, which have also been active in branch extension, have improved their positions in regard to profits. On the other hand, the National, Union, and Clydesdale Banks have been less active in planting branches, and the first has increased profits, the second has decreased profits, and the third shows but slight improvement. Thus, although branch extension is undertaken for the express purpose of maintaining and extending business, and is therefore vitally associated with profit experience, either the activity has been sometimes misplaced, or other influences have been so powerful as to obliterate the traces of the results.

But perhaps the question may be viewed from another standpoint. If we examine into the amount of profit drawn, on an average, from each office open in 1865 and 1896, it is found that a very large falling off has occurred. In the former year the amount per office (including the Central and City Banks) was £1709, while now it is only £1267; a decline which was almost steady, at about £18 per annum until last year's improvement in earnings was shown. As it is, the decrease averages £14 per annum. This experience has been general with the banks, but they have been affected in different degrees. It is not easy to draw any conclusive deductions from the various experiences; but it would seem as if those banks whose branch systems have been oldest established were suffering least. Thus we find that the Commercial, National, and Union, which have been comparatively quiescent in the matter of branch extension during the period under review, are all under average in the falling off. On the

PROFITS PER OFFICE OPEN.

Bank.	1865.	1872.	1883.	1895.	1896.	Loss per Office.	Rate of Loss per Annum.	
							1865-95.	1865-96.
Bank - - - - - - -	£2273	£1834	£1706	£1332	£1364	£909	£31½	£28⅓
Royal - - - - - -	2373	1972	1680	1282	1314	1059	36¼	33
British - - - - - -	2861	2392	1485	1698	1813	1048	38¾	32¾
Commercial - - -	1700	1737	1326	1234	†1448	252	15½	†8
National - - - - -	1810	1914	1844	1459	1636	174	11¾	5½
Union - - - - - -	1410	1253	1166	865	1033	377	18	11¾
Clydesdale - - - - -	1838	1832	1255	1083	1187	651	25	20⅓
Town and County -	954	701	628	545	585	369	13½	11½
North of Scotland -	1099	965	768	589	638	461	17	14⅓
Caledonian - - - - -	*1364	*1361	552	524	547	817	28	25½
Central - - - - - -	1250	—	—	—	—	—	—	—
City - - - - - - -	944	862	—	—	—	—	—	—
Averages - - - - - -	£1709	£1563	£1362	£1161	£1267	£442	£18¼	£13¾

* Profits exceptional. † Ten branches withdrawn.

other hand the three old banks, which in 1865 were head
and shoulders above the others in amount of profit per
office, and have since been active in branch extension,
show a falling off twice as great. The two Aberdeen
banks, whose systems were early established, also show
under average falling off. But this theory will hardly
meet all the difficulties of the question.

To investigate the influences affecting the profit experiences of the banks would be a most interesting and vitally instructive work, but it would require more detailed information and intimate knowledge of the affairs of the various banks than is obtainable from published reports. It does, indeed, appear that conservatism in division of profit is associated with prosperity; but, on the other hand, the Union, North of Scotland, and Caledonian Banks, which all stand high in this respect, have all had adverse experiences; while the British Linen, Commercial, and Town and County Banks, which occupy to some extent a medium position, have been comparatively prosperous. Perhaps it depends to a considerable extent on the earliness, continuity, and thoroughness of the practice of the policy. But this will not wholly solve the problem. The conduct of all business is associated with questions of *personnel*, mental, social, and even physical conditions, and that host of undefinable minor qualities and actions which influence all the relationships of life.

As banks exist not only for the benefit of the community, but also for the profit of the adventurers (as they used to be most logically called), it is fitting at this point of our investigation to consider how far the general policy of each bank has been to the advantage of the proprietors. Of course the actual day-to-day management of a bank enters largely into the results of its experience; but it is obviously impossible to take such considerations into account in this connection. It must be assumed that each of the banks has been conducted to the best advantage of its constituents, both private and public, that its special circumstances would permit of. It must also be borne in mind that the results do not necessarily follow from the policy pursued during the years embraced in our survey, but may, to a greater or less extent, depend on the policy of former years. In pursuing this investigation it will not be sufficient to look solely at the rate of dividend now payable, but rather at the return obtainable on the aggregate amount of the proprietors' funds. In this view the Commercial and National Banks have, among the large banks, held leading places all through the thirty years; but whereas the National had slightly the lead up till 1883, the Commercial has since distanced it, and now stands first among the banks for the return made to the proprietors on the private liabilities of the bank. The two Aberdeen banks have also done very well in this respect, although the North of Scotland has recently been handicapped by its vigorous efforts to replace its losses in the fishing trade. The three old banks have not improved their positions—the Bank of Scotland, which was first in 1865 with 11 per cent., being now fourth with 7 per cent., and the others having fallen off in lesser degrees. Of course, conservatism in the division of profit, and efforts to strengthen the guarantees to the public, tend to lessen the return to proprietors. But while a general lessening of the return is shown, it appears that the more conservative members of the family are able to give a better return to proprietors than those that have reserved a smaller portion of their profits. That is to say, the British Linen, Town and County, Bank of Scotland, National, and Commercial Banks, which have done most to strengthen their private funds, are also those which give the best return to the proprietors, although they come in somewhat different order in the latter aspect. Of course, profits reserved are not lost to the shareholders, but, being employed in the business, earn profit which swells the general return.

DIVIDEND TO PROPRIETORS' FUNDS.

Bank.	1865. Per Cent.	1872. Per Cent.	1883. Per Cent.	1896. Per Cent.	Better or Worse. Per Cent.
Bank	11	8·6	7·9	7·0	− 4·0
Royal	6	6·7	6·9	5·6	− 0·4
British	8	9·1	7·6	6·9	− 1·1
Commercial	8	9·6	8·6	8·3	+ 0·3
National	8	9·7	8·7	7·8	− 0·2
Union	6	8·9	7·9	5·9	− 0·1
Clydesdale	7	8·8	7·1	6·2	− 0·8
Town and County	7	7·8	7·9	7·6	+ 0·6
North of Scotland	7	7·9	7·7	5·3	− 1·7
Caledonian	5	8·4	5·3	5·2	+ 0·2
Central	7	—	—	—	—
City	8	8·1	—	—	—
	7·6	9·4	7·5	6·6	− 1·0

The question of the profitableness of the banking business may also be examined from the point of view of the return obtained from the use of borrowed funds. For the purposes of this examination we allow 4 per cent. in 1865 and 3 per cent. in 1895 as proportion of profits applicable to the proprietors' funds. The remainder of the profits may be considered as derivable from the public liabilities. On this basis the average return to the ten banks in 1865 was 1·1 per cent., and among the banks individually the rates conformed with reasonable closeness to the general average. The north country banks showed higher rates than most of the large banks. Among the latter the British Linen had the highest rate, 1·23 per cent., and the Royal Bank the lowest, 0·90 per cent. Turning to 1895, we find that the general average fell, notwithstanding the lower rate we have allowed on proprietors' funds, to 0·66 per cent. The banks conformed in the same degree to the general average, but changed places to some extent. The British Linen, however, still occupies the chief place, closely followed by the Commercial. The Town and County, Clydesdale, and North of Scotland Banks are also over the average, while the National is but little under it. One of the striking features is the apparent low profit earning rates of the Bank of Scotland, Royal Bank, and Union Bank, which bring up the rear with little more than ½ per cent. The increased profits declared last year bring up the general average to 0·74 per cent.

As a companion table to that appended to our last chapter, we give the following view of the relative positions of the banks as regards progress on the combined bases of improvement in (1) proprietors' funds, (2) deposits, (3) advances, (4) banking reserves, (5) amount written off property, (6) new branches, and (7) profit experience :—

RELATIVE POSITIONS AS REGARDS PROGRESS.

Name.	1865-72.	1872-83.	1883-95.	1895-96.	Better + Worse −
Bank - - - -	5	1	3	3	+ 2
Royal - - - -	7	7	10	10	− 3
British - - -	10	5	2	2	+ 8
Commercial - -	4	8	4	4	0
National - - -	2	4	7	6	− 4
Union - - -	9	9	9	9	0
Clydesdale - -	1	3	6	5	− 4
Town & County	6	6	1	1	+ 5
North of Scot. -	8	2	5	7	+ 1
Caledonian - -	3	10	8	8	− 5

From this it appears that the British Linen Company, the two Aberdeen banks, and the Bank of Scotland have improved their relative positions; the Commercial and Union Banks have maintained their places in the race; while the others have advanced at less rapid rates.

PROFITS ON PUBLIC LIABILITIES.

Bank.	1865. Per Cent.	1895. Per Cent.	1896. Per Cent.	Fall. Per Cent.
Bank	1·17	0·55	0·57	0·60
Royal	0·90	0·54	0·56	0·34
British	1·23	0·87	0·96	0·27
Commercial	0·95	0·81	0·90	0·05
National	0·94	0·64	0·72	0·22
Union	1·10	0·54	0·72	0·38
Clydesdale	1·20	0·68	0·75	0·45
Town and County	1·61	0·80	0·89	0·72
North of Scotland	1·21	0·66	0·73	0·48
Caledonian	*2·07	0·60	0·66	1·41
	1·10	0·66	0·74	0·36

There remains to be noticed the loss experience of the banks. But at the outset we are met with this difficulty, that it is comparatively rarely that any specification of loss is made, the usual practice being to declare the net profits after making "ample provision for all bad and doubtful debts". The only gauge by which to estimate the ordinary annual loss is that already referred to, wherein the losses of the Royal Bank from 1865 to 1874 inclusive are shown to have averaged 1s. 1¼d. per cent. per annum. That that experience was an unusually favourable one is indicated by the facts that it was received with surprise at the time, and that no other bank has offered to cap it. But as it would be merely guessing to attempt to amend it, we must accept it as the standard

* Profits exceptional. 1·3 per cent. on basis of 1866 and 1867.

for the general experience. On this basis, then, the ordinary losses during the thirty years would be about £1,100,000. This, as we have pointed out, must be deemed a moderate estimate. But there falls to be added to it the losses specified in the annual reports, amounting in all to nearly £800,000. And lastly, we must include the City of Glasgow Bank's losses to the extent of £6,640,983. We thus ascertain a total loss experience of £8,500,000 sterling in thirty years. This gives a yearly average of loss to the extent of about £284,500. It may be objected that to include the City Bank's losses is unfair, as these were exceptional. But we are dealing with the actual experience of banking in Scotland, and must therefore include all losses by bad debts, whether exceptionally large or not. Besides, it is questionable if we are entitled to assume that the City Bank disaster was exceptional. The immediately preceding generation witnessed a similar exceptional disaster proportionate to the development of business at that time. The generation before that again suffered from several minor failures, and its immediate predecessor was still more unfortunate. The generation preceding that sustained the Ayr Bank collapse and a multiplicity of smaller failures. As this takes us back to the period of the commencement of the developed banking system, it is apparent that it would be unsafe to treat any loss as outside the normal experience. But, excluding this special element, the average annual loss would appear to be about £63,000. It is not, however, the actual amount of loss that is of so much consequence as the extent of the provision made for it in anticipation. And in this view it is pleasing to find that five of the banks—the Bank of Scotland, the British Linen, Commercial, National, and Town and County — have not required during the whole thirty years to trouble the proprietors with any specific announcement as to provision for losses, while all the others satisfactorily met the necessities as they occurred. It is noticeable, however, that most of those which are in the former category have been conservative in the division of profits; while those which have had to confess to special losses have all paid higher rates of dividend than they pay now. If these latter had only estimated the contingencies of the future at a somewhat higher rate, we might have had a clean slate in the matter of recorded losses.

In concluding our review of Scottish banking during the last three decades, the question naturally arises, "What will the future be?" To answer it is, of course, impossible. But as the best guide to the future is a study of the past, we can deduce from the experiences which we have been examining and the conditions which we find in existence what the general tendency of the course of events is likely to be. In the first place, it would appear that the rate of interest is on the down grade. There will doubtless be improvement from time to time, as there has been recently, but there seems no reason to hope that the next thirty years will give anything like as good an average as the last thirty. Of course some great disturbing element, involving great consumption of capital, such as a European war, might alter the condition of affairs, at least for a time; but, barring unforeseen contingencies, the normal profit capabilities of banking may be expected to decline. State interference is also an adverse factor to be included in such considerations. Moreover, in our advancing state of civilisation, financial and mercantile developments tend to produce conditions of greater danger, so that provision for losses behoves to be on a larger scale than formerly, to the further restriction of profits. Of course adjustments of rates may be made from time to time; but the lower deposit rates fall the greater is the danger of killing the goose that lays the golden eggs. The field of business may, as we have hinted, be widened; but every new enterprise is attended by dangers peculiar to itself. Besides, the force of circumstances is sufficiently abrogating the old traditions without such additional revolutionary change. Well is it with those banks which have made the affluence of the past minister to the necessities of the future! If the anticipation of evil should prove true, they will rise lightly to the waves of adversity; should the expectation be agreeably disappointed, their voyage will be but the more prosperous.

CHAPTER V.

PROVISION FOR LOSSES.*

ONE of the most important phrases constantly occurring in bank reports is that which usually accompanies the statement of the amount of net profit made during the period under review. The City of Glasgow Bank, occupying as it did an exceptional position among banks, latterly dispensed with the practice; but it is an almost invariable rule to declare the profits as ascertained "after provision for all bad and doubtful debts". Where this assurance is not given attention should at once be called to the omission. There are great differences, however, in the practice of banks in making such provision. While it is a recognised custom to make an estimate of prospective losses, and to deduct from the profits the amount so required, some banks probably err in minimising their loss. There is a great temptation to this in the case of young banks, even in cases where the general management may be otherwise good; and, of course, where banks have got into a weak condition, the temptation is still stronger. In the case of old-established and wealthy banks, a contrary course is usually followed. It is felt as a relief to cut out all doubtful business when ascertaining the position of the establishment. In this way it often comes about that excessive provision for losses is made. While this may

* *North British Economist*, Nov., 1894.

seem to infringe the rights of the proprietors, it is truly the wisest course that can be followed. The position of a bank should always be actually better than it is represented to be by published statements. An invisible reserve is thus created, which in times of pressure forms an admirable buffer between the bank and adverse experience.

The reserve fund is often called a provision for losses. It is so undoubtedly. Before the capital can be encroached on, it must disappear. But it should very rarely occur that any deduction from the reserve fund requires to be made. When such a transference is made, a bank's credit is undoubtedly injured in somewhat the same way as if its capital were reduced. In point of fact, the accumulation of a reserve fund is in one sense an increase of capital. If dividends are not paid on it nominally, it is at least earning profit which permits a higher dividend to be paid on what is technically called the capital. If, then, a reduction of the reserve fund is injurious to the credit of a bank, it is right that special care should be taken to avoid such a contingency. But bad debts are inseparable from the business of banking. A bank that refused to run any risk would not get current business, and would become a mere investment company. Consequently they should be regarded as a necessary part of the business, and treated accordingly in the general policy of management. Unfortunately, however, bad debts in banking experience are like comets in the solar system. While they may be expected with absolute certainty, the time and manner of their arrival, their number and their magnitude, are often involved in impenetrable uncertainty. Considerable periods may elapse without any material loss emerging. At other times losses occur with irksome repetition. There are times for small losses, and times for big ones. Careful management will, of course, minimise the amount of loss experienced; but it often happens that the strongest banks suffer very severely. The case of the London and Westminster Bank is a case in point. With more than £30,000,000 of assets its directors have sometimes been able to say that no loss of any consequence had been made during half a year's business. And yet to those who remember the time of the arch-swindler Collie, such statements recall a startling experience, which has long since been recovered from, and which even at the time was borne with ease owing to the ample provision made previously for unusual contingencies, but which was accompanied with very serious anxiety and grievous loss.

But while it is right year by year to lay aside privately from profits a sum sufficient to cover all foreseen possible losses, there is another class of losses which should also be provided for in the same way. These are the unforeseen losses—those which are not expected, but inevitably come. It is, for the most part, only in good years that this can be done. If not done when large profits are being earned, and when losses are agreeably conspicuous by their absence, it becomes necessary to do it when profits are small and losses are numerous. In other words, bank profits should be estimated not by the year, but by tens of years. The profits, in excess of the average, gained in good years, will thus make up for the deficient profits of bad years. Such a policy as this has a splendid effect on the credit of a bank. When it is seen to ride out a financial storm without losing a spar, it is regarded with almost boundless confidence. It is, moreover, too often forgotten by shareholders that profits reserved are not lost to them. The money still remains their property, is probably in safer keeping than in their own, is earning profit for them, and is ensuring them from future danger.

These remarks are applicable to other businesses than banking. Had such a policy as we are here advocating been followed out by property and other investment companies, their recent experiences would in all likelihood have been avoided. To the public it would all along have seemed as though their profits were on a moderate scale; consequently, there would have been less competition and less speculative business. When the bad times came they would have been able to meet their losses without such apparent serious consequences as have been seen. It is a safe rule for all companies trading on credit to dispense entirely with sanguineness, to estimate profits as less than they appear to be, and to treat losses as larger than they are likely to prove. Another point to be noticed is the effect of the reduction of dividend owing to provision for losses. It is often said that this hurts a bank's credit. No doubt, as we have seen, it is best to be provided beforehand with minor reserves. But, should the loss exceed the amount of the provision, a reduction of dividend to meet the deficiency is only regarded as prudence. The market price of the stock falls, but the credit of the institution is uninjured. Only in cases where doubt exists in the public mind as to the fulness of the provision, is any damage done to credit. But this aspect of the case shows all the more conclusively the advisableness of being forearmed against the necessity for declaring losses at all.

CHAPTER VI.

BANK NOTE ISSUES.*

IN all discussions on banking the question of note issues takes a leading place. This is the natural result of association of ideas in the public mind. Every one has practical knowledge of bank notes, while comparatively few persons have accurate acquaintance with the nature of banking operations, or of the principles on which these are conducted. This state of matters was strikingly evidenced by the character of the recent discussion regarding the Scotch banks in the correspondence column of the *Scotsman*, where many of the writers indulged in wild statements and in crude suggestions at which practical bankers could only smile. But while it is natural that the subject of bank notes should bulk largely in the public eye, seeing they form a very great proportion of the currency of the United Kingdom, and in Scotland and Ireland take the place of gold almost entirely, it is yet somewhat extraordinary that economists and financiers should follow suit to so great an extent as they do. In connection with currency investigations the subject assumes a vital interest; but in regard to banking it is quite of secondary importance. The bank note circulation of the United Kingdom is about £43,500,000 sterling, of which about £35,500,000 is backed by tangible security,

* *Scottish Banking and Insurance Magazine*, 1st Nov., 1880.

leaving about £8,000,000 based purely on credit. Now the daily average of cheques, bills, etc., passed through the London Clearing House alone is fully £16,000,000.* That is to say that there is continually in circulation through the one channel of the London Bankers' Clearing House twice as much unsecured paper drawn by the customers of the various banks as there is of bank notes in circulation throughout the kingdom above the required provision of securities and bullion. Again, if we compare the deposit and note liabilities of the banks, a still stronger case is made out. Confining ourselves to Scotland (as English and Irish statistics are defective), it will be found that last year the banks in Scotland held upwards of £73,000,000 of deposited money as contrasted with a liability of about £5,500,000 on account of notes in the hands of the public.† The acceptances of the banks, which are always regarded as the highest class of paper, and circulate freely without question as to special security, sometimes exceed the amount of the note issues. It is thus apparent that the note circulation is trifling in amount in comparison with the other public liabilities of the banks, and with the currency liabilities of their customers.

In its essential characteristics a bank note does not differ materially from other transferable demand documents, as the fundamental function of each is the instantaneous transference of a right to a specific sum of standard coin. But from force of habit, formed through experience of convenience, bank notes have for long been regarded as money, although they are merely a substitute for it. In consequence of the extent to which this popular conception

---

* Now nearly £21,000,000.
† Now £95,750,000 and £7,250,000 respectively.

has attained, the Legislature has wisely taken special precautions for the regulation of bank issues. We do not say that their provisions have always been judicious, but there was a manifest reason for their assuming particular control over this species of currency. Hitherto, however, Parliament has tacitly recognised the right of issue, although it has restricted the exercise of that right in such ways as it deemed advisable in the public interest. The view that the right to issue and make profit by paper currency is one of the peculiar prerogatives of the State, has for long found many advocates, but it has never been adopted by the British Legislature. The foundation of this opinion is that, as notes are substitutes generally accepted for the coin of the realm, and as the control of metallic currency is the prerogative of the State, the paper currency should also be in the hands of the State. It has, however, been repeatedly shown by economists that there is a distinct fallacy in this argument. The metallic currency is not and never has been, strictly speaking, in the hands of Government. Any one who has command of gold bullion can issue it in the form of coin; but, in order to secure the lieges against imposition, it is required that his bullion should receive the imprimatur of the Crown. Similarly, as bank notes have acquired a public recognition as currency, Parliament has assumed a certain amount of control on their issue. Some states have assumed the right of issuing paper currency, but in every case it has proved injurious to the public interest, for the tendency of government issues to become inconvertible is, in times of financial pressure, too strong to be resisted, and inconvertibility destroys the essential characteristic of a proper paper currency as an efficient and economical substitute for coin.

It is a popular belief that the note issues are a great source of direct profit to the banks. Thus, when it is stated that the Bank of Scotland has an average circulation of upwards of £800,000,* it is often supposed that that is as good to the bank as money deposited without interest. So far from this being actually the case, it is somewhat doubtful if there is any profit from the transaction. It is only on the sum of £343,418 that the bank can make any profit at all. For the remaining portion of its issue it must keep a corresponding amount of bullion. That represents a complete loss of interest. From the income derivable from the authorised issue there falls to be deducted the expense of manufacturing the entire body of notes—a very heavy item—Government duty, bankers' licences, charges for conveyance of bullion, exchange expenses, and a multiplicity of minor outlays. From this it will readily be seen that there is small room for direct profit to any of the banks, and none whatever to those whose authorised issues are small in proportion to their actual circulation. The direct profit on bank note issues goes principally to Government in the shape of saving in wear and tear of the gold coin, and in special taxation.

It is not to be supposed, however, that the banks derive little or no advantage from the right of issue. We have just shown that the direct advantages are small; but if we turn to the indirect advantages they will be found to be considerable. We are here speaking of the Scotch and Irish banks—the English country note issues have been quite paralysed. The one great advantage to be derived from the power of issue appertains to the notes as still unissued, not to those in the hands of the public. From

* Now £1,000,000.

those in active circulation the banks get but little if any profit; from those ready to be issued they derive a great advantage. Were it not for the power to issue notes, and the readiness with which the public receive them, the banks could never have afforded to open a third of the branches which have been established. The reason for this is a very simple one. Without the right of issue a bank must, at every one of its offices, hold the whole of its balance of cash in the shape of coin, or of notes of other banks, which, as far as it is concerned, are as unprofitable as coin. Such balances entail a complete loss of interest which can only be borne where the amount of business is of considerable extent. There are probably not above one (at most two) hundred localities in Scotland that would satisfy such conditions. When, however, a bank can hold its till-money in the shape of notes, it is enabled to extend its operations into districts which otherwise would be quite inaccessible. It is for this reason, and for this almost entirely, that the Scotch banks have been able to develop their branch systems to an extent that has made Scotland notable as having the greatest supply of bank offices in proportion to population of all the countries in the world. The opponents of bank issues must lay their account to witnessing a great contraction in the number of bank offices, or alternatively a great increase in provincial bank charges. It is thus apparent that the public are even more interested in preserving the *status quo* than the banks themselves.

On former occasions the public of Scotland have, with shrewd sense, preserved this powerful agency for the maintenance of their commercial prosperity, against the views of Government. These views are, to all appearance, still held by the majority of British statesmen, and always tend to assert themselves; for in England, which is the dominant unit of the Union, banking has been stereotyped in a much less developed form than in Scotland, through pernicious legislation. But in Scotland, where banking has matured into a natural and thoroughly economic form, it behoves the public to be on their guard against encroachments on those elements of banking which have been efficient aids in establishing its prosperity. The banks will always be able to look after their own interests, for they will never long continue an unprofitable course of business; but the public may be entrapped by popular agitation into the thraldom which has been the aim of statesmen since the days of Sir Robert Peel.

CHAPTER VII.

THE ULTIMATE GOLD RESERVE.

ONE of the few unsolved problems in British banking is the provision and maintenance of a bullion reserve suited to the extended and ever-extending character of the banking system, the commercial and mercantile business, and the national and imperial interests. British credit is, as has often been pointed out, based on but a slender foundation of hard cash. There is not in this an accusation of inflation. From time to time, no doubt, financial or mercantile inflation does occur, with its sequel of panic and crisis. But, with these occasional excrescences, British credit is based on a stronger foundation of actual exchangeable wealth than any other nation, ancient or modern, could show. Nevertheless, the position of private and national credit is one of great danger, which only the extreme robustness of our national constitution enables us to ignore. But, as the strongest man is but a child in the whirlwind, so the robustest national credit might snap in a conjunction of unfavourable international contingencies.

Our temerity in the matter of bullion reserves will best be comprehended by a comparison of the British position with that of the other great powers. While our reserve of bullion, largely increased within recent years, represented by the coined and uncoined gold and (to a small extent) silver in the Bank of England, is round about £35,000,000, the stock of gold in the Bank of France is equivalent to about £80,000,000, besides which they hold silver to the value (nominal) of £50,000,000. The Imperial Bank of Germany and the Austro-Hungarian Bank together hold coin and bullion to the value of £85,000,000; while the Bank of Russia has a stock amounting to £96,500,000, of which less than £4,000,000 consists of silver. It may be argued that the note issues of these banks are much larger than the circulation of the Bank of England. But, on the other hand, that fact is of comparatively little importance, as convertibility is not an essential doctrine in these countries as it is with us, while in the case of Russia there is an actual condition of inconvertibility. But not only are those banks so much stronger than our national establishment, they are not so subject to foreign drains as we are. Owing to the autocratic tone of continental (even republican) governments they are enabled to retain their stocks when they deem it unadvisable to part with any. Even in Germany, where there are several banks of issue, the moral influence of the central establishment, when it is found necessary to exercise it, is powerful enough to restrain all the local banks from reducing their metallic reserves. This is in itself equivalent to an additional reserve of coin; as it is no doubt intended to be.

Since the passing of the Bank Act of 1844 [*] there has been an ever-growing feeling of dissatisfaction, or at least uneasiness, with regard to the monetary system which was then instituted. From time to time the discussion of

[*] This and two following paragraphs from *Edinburgh Courant*, 9th Jan, 1875.

its merits and demerits becomes so animated, and the disturbance of the money market under its provisions has become so frequent, that new legislation on the subject is called for. But, unfortunately, as usually happens in public discussions, the would-be reformers are by no means agreed as to what course it would be well to follow. A proposal was made in the columns of the *Economist*, by an eminent financier, for the formation, by the clearing bankers, of a cash reserve under their own custody, by the withdrawal of their balances from the Bank of England, to the extent of £8,000,000. This plan met with much adverse criticism, which was doubtless quite deserved, as it is evident that, whatever advantage it might bring to the clearing bankers, it would not increase the banking reserve of the nation, and the scheme thus failed to mitigate the situation. But other suggested schemes, if more extensive, and seemingly complete, have not commended themselves as calculated to be any more efficacious, while they would probably entail many evil consequences; and some are, indeed, founded on incorrect financial theories, which is not the case with the former.

The opinions of a section of reformers, who may be called the Radicals of the financial world, were embodied, with considerable force and ability, in a pamphlet which was published some time ago, by an English banker. After justly pointing out the error of the comparatively small amount of attention given by the general public to monetary questions, the author goes on to lament that the Bank of England should have, to so great an extent, lost the control of the money market, while its bullion reserve is so small that the withdrawal of even £1,000,000 tends to raise the discount rate; and that the cash balances of the other banks are so disproportioned to their deposit liabilities. He suggests as a remedy that the Act of 1844 should be repealed, that all bank note issues should be abolished, and that the Government should issue a national paper currency. These proposals are not new; indeed they have been made and refuted again and again; but with an extraordinary persistency they crop up whenever there is a discussion upon currency. With all its faults, the Act of 1844 is not to be so lightly disposed of; and although the centralisation of note issues was a leading object with its framers, more recent discussion has shown the unadvisableness of such a proceeding; and very little study is required to discover the fallacy of arguments in favour of Government taking the note issues into its own hands.

The issuing of notes by banks is much more economical and convenient for the nation than a state issue would be; and, although in some cases the latter ways have been quite successful, in others the consequences have been very disastrous. Besides, while sometimes necessary, it is a dangerous power to place in the hands of a government. The conjunction, on the other hand, of the issue of notes with general banking business gives a reciprocal advantage to each department such as cannot be obtained when they are dissociated. What would our Scottish banks have been without their note issues? What, indeed, would Scotland have been without them? It was the notes that cultivated the land, caught the fish on the coasts, and developed the trade and commerce of the country; thus producing the deposits which have enabled the banks to bring their advantages within the reach of every one. Take away their liberty to issue notes, and the Scottish banks must withdraw many of their branches, increase their charges, and perhaps even reduce their deposit interest rates. An extension of freedom to issue notes, under proper conditions to secure convertibility, would be a much more advantageous arrangement for the nation, than a curtailment of the right.

The only practical contribution from Scotland towards the discussion of this subject was contained in an address by Mr. Charles Gairdner, of the Union Bank of Scotland, to the London Institute of Bankers, in February, 1886.* Basing his theories on the experience of banking in Scotland, he endeavoured to show how the scarcity of gold, which is complained of by some economists, might be mitigated by greater economy in the use of that metal for currency purposes. It is well known that the currency of Scotland differs from that of England in so far as the banks of the former country are permitted to issue notes of the value of £1, while no notes of a lower denomination than £5 are permitted south of the Tweed. The consequence of this is, that in Scotland sovereigns are comparatively little used; while in England they form a very large portion of the currency. Now Mr. Gairdner sought to show that by the adoption of the Scottish system of £1 notes, the gold supply of the nation would be practically increased by the amount of sovereigns liberated from their present currency function. With sufficient provision for the convertibility of the notes, a paper currency is greatly more economical than a metallic currency. The wear and tear of a soft metal, such as gold, is in itself a serious item in the consumption, not only on account of the amount, but

* This and the four following paragraphs were published in 1886.

because, unlike the other items of consumption, the metal thus lost is lost for ever.

But it is the still greater economy which might be secured by permitting the gold displaced by paper to be used for other purposes, such as international exchanges, that Mr. Gairdner chiefly points to. In this connection he estimates that £50,000,000 might be liberated. This is probably not an over-estimate, when the total gold currency is taken at £120,000,000. But it must be remembered that under the present system this amount would simply be transferred to the vaults of the Bank of England, and not added to the available gold supply. For as the accepted theory is, that paper currency must be based on gold, for every £1 note which left the bank one sovereign would have to go in. Mr. Gairdner seems to hint, however, at an alteration of the law, whereby one half of the increased note issues might be founded on securities. This presupposes a change in legislative principles which is probably not practicable at present. But even if £25,000,000 were thus made available, does Mr. Gairdner's theory hold good that our trade would be benefited as by the creation of a hundred new capitalists each with £250,000? If the scarcity of gold actually exists, it exists all over the world; and as gold finds its level among civilised nations as surely as water does in nature, would not the increased supply be distributed among at least the gold-currency nations? If so, Britain would only retain that portion applicable to its own relative position in the world.

But is it true that there is a scarcity of gold? It is undoubted that there is a diminished yearly supply; * but

* This was written before the great South African influx.

may there not also be a diminished yearly demand? Economies in the use of gold have been continually increasing, although the special economy advocated by Mr. Gairdner has not received the attention it deserves. The system of cheques, bankers' railway and other clearings and exchanges are being more and more extended and perfected. With lower prices and decreased expenditure on the necessaries and comforts, as well as on the luxuries of life consequent on the diminution of incomes, the consumption of gold must be less, while a decreasing volume of trade values year by year over the world will make smaller demands on the gold supply. This, of course, is hypothesis; but what say the Bank of England returns? It has hitherto been held that a scarcity of gold involved a drain on the bank, which in its turn occasioned a high discount rate. But instead of money being dearer, it has for years been abnormally cheap; and the supposititious seekers after gold ignore the heaps in the bank which are obtainable on demand. This seems inconsistent with an unsatisfied desire for gold by the outside world.

Without absolutely denying that there is a scarcity of currency—the testimony of so many able economists in favour of the theory is not to be lightly put aside—there yet seem to be many reasons for doubting its existence, or at least for thinking that its effects are not so direct as some theorists would have us believe.* Of course an inadequate supply of gold, other things being the same, implies a fall in prices; for if there is less of it, more commodities must be given in exchange for it. But other circumstances may counteract the deficit. When Mr.

* The scarcity theory was much more strongly held in 1886 than it is now.

Gairdner speaks of there being perhaps both a fall in the prices of commodities, and an appreciation of gold, we are further involved in a speculation to which there appear no bounds. It is sufficiently difficult to compare a variety of fluctuating prices (commodities), on the one hand, with another fluctuating price (gold) taken as a standard, on the other, and to determine which has altered its position. But when we are asked to consider both sides of the comparison as fluctuating, we are entitled to demand a new standard. When silver was practically stationary in value, it may have been a fairly trustworthy measure; but whatever may have been its utility in that respect in former times, it is, for such a purpose, worse than useless now; and no substitute is offered to us.

Again, Mr. Gairdner seems to imply, although he does not say so, that a low range of prices is an evil; and this is practically involved in the position of all those economists who are deploring the decrease in the gold supply. The trade theory is that high prices and prosperity, and low prices and depression, go hand in hand. And it is, so far, quite true. When prices fall to such a point that there is not sufficient profit for the producers and distributers of goods, the condition of trade is to be deplored. But, on the other hand, when prices rise so that consumers are straitened to supply the superfluities of producers, there is cause both of regret and anxiety. Now it must not be forgotten that, after all, the greatest good of the greatest number is secured by moderate prices. This is really the principle of free trade, which enables consumers to buy the produce of all the world at the cheapest rates. Even when trade is bad, and employment scarce, low prices mitigate the suffering. We have lately [1886] heard much of the prospects of the Mysore and other Indian gold mines; but, if expectations are realised, and they pour their riches on the world, will the chief result be a rise in prices? Or will dear commodities be accompanied by expanding trade and plenty of employment at high wages? Or are the fluctuations in the relative values of gold and commodities simply oscillations which preserve the equilibrium, without indicating any direct influence of the supplies of gold on the condition of trade?

The great error of those who have propounded schemes for the strengthening of the bullion reserve has been the attempt to devise a system which will not involve loss of interest. Ultimately, however, the banks generally recognised the necessity for practical action, and agreed to keep larger balances than formerly at their credit with the Bank of England, to enable that institution to maintain its reserve at higher points. Towards this movement, the state of the money market was, no doubt, a contributing element; as the large accumulations of floating balances made the sacrifice less than it would have been formerly. Nay, there may have been little if any sacrifice, for by lessening the competition of loanable capital they tended to improve discount rates. It is here, however, that the weakness of the system appears. The plan is good, and just, so far as it goes. The result is not only satisfactory, but the mutual action of the banks in sharing the responsibility of maintaining the reserve, places the burden more equitably than formerly. But the weakness exists in the temptation under which the banks lie to reduce their balances when the demand for accommodation increases during periods of trade or speculative activity. Such periods are usually followed by times of more or less acute crisis, when the strength of the reserve is an all-important matter. Besides, the banks might be compelled to draw on their balances in self-protection. But even if that should not occur, the gold might be drained away despite the efforts of all combined. But even if the banks, or most of them, prove conscientious enough to resist the temptation to reduce their balances with the Bank of England, and the reserve be maintained sufficiently for trade and general business requirements, there still remains the danger of international complications; a contingency which does not seem ever to have received that amount of consideration which its importance deserves.

If the problem of putting the ultimate gold reserve on a satisfactory footing is ever to be thoroughly solved, it can only be by governmental action. To put the burden on the Bank of England alone, is tacitly acknowledged to be unjust. On the other hand, mutual agreements are apt to break down when the necessity for them is greatest. Besides, improved as the state of the reserves has been since the conjoint recognition of individual responsibility, it can hardly be held that, from a national point of view, the position is all that is desirable. But any material increase of effort on the part of the banks cannot be looked for. It follows, then, that any further step must be taken, if taken at all, at the expense of the nation. The cost would, doubtless, be considerable. An additional reserve of less than £10,000,000 would hardly be thought of; but the interest on that sum at $2\frac{1}{2}$ per cent. would amount to £250,000 per annum; enough to make any Chancellor of the Exchequer shake his head. All the same, it is a question if it might not be true economy to secure financial salvation at such an outlay.

But the expense might be mitigated. The simplest plan would be to keep the gold at the Bank of England, but under the exclusive control of the Treasury. There might also be provision for an issue of notes (based on the stock of gold) under special conditions, to meet occasional and temporary requirements. Some portion of the Government balances, usually amounting to several millions, might be devoted towards providing and maintaining the reserve. On those occasions when that portion of the Treasury balances might require to be drawn on, notes (say of large denomination, to secure that their currency should not be unduly prolonged) might be issued. Otherwise, recourse would be had to the money market, where any desired amount could be had on easy terms, or the assistance of the bank would be invoked *pro tempore*, or such portion of the gold itself as might be necessary transferred to the bank. Similarly in times of crisis, notes based on the national gold reserve might be issued to supplement those of the Bank of England; thus tending to obviate the necessity for those violations of the Act of 1844 which, while justifiable, are by no means good form. Of course such a scheme would require the most careful and expert consideration; and would necessitate minute arrangement of details by those specially conversant with the departments concerned. But it seems possible, if the national obligation were recognised, that an efficient and fairly economical system of gold reserves might be established and maintained. The expense involved might be readily far more than recouped by the mitigation of the acuteness of periodically recurring crises; and, as a species of national protection, such a reserve might be hardly less important than our nominal defences.

CHAPTER VIII.

EVOLUTION.

" Stands Scotland where it did."
—*Macbeth.*

THE lapse of a period of time which is usually termed a generation has, as we have seen in the course of our survey of the business aspects of our subject, produced great changes both in the character and conduct of Scottish banking. But the changes do not stop there. The tone and personality of the profession are largely altered. The banker of to-day is no more like his predecessor of the sixties, than the west-end advocate of to-day is like Mr. Counsellor Pleydell. The old Scottish banker was a most interesting, albeit not usually a very lovable character. Cold-blooded, cool-headed, canny, with, perchance, a dash of pawkiness; he was at his best in his office. If he shone elsewhere at all it was in church affairs. But the concentration of his interest was in his business. His bank either was superior to all the others, or he intended to make it so. He was content with what would now be deemed poor pay; but in truth he did not work for remuneration (that was a mere accompaniment of his duties), but with self-devotion to the one absorbing passion of his life, the welfare and aggrandisement of his beloved establishment. He was not by any means indifferent to his personal financial interests, but he was of the same genus as the private banker, identifying his own with his bank's interests.

A *fin de siècle* business man can hardly appreciate the old banker's frame of mind. To him work is self-interest, and devotion is only justified by its pecuniary results; to the other his bank's interests were as dear as if the establishment were his private property. Perhaps this arose to some extent from the more isolated and provincial condition of the Scotland of that day. At all events business conditions used to be more simple, and the banker was more directly in touch, not only with his own customers, but with the community. He knew all who had or might have dealings with him, so far as their responsibility went. He could tell Jack McQuirk from Sandy Canny without telephoning to have the "Mc" and "C" card drawers examined; and Jack got the right-about whenever he put his head in at the door, while Sandy was bowed into an arm-chair before he had overcome his trepidation at crossing the threshold of capital. But a change has come with the keener struggle of competition, the wider range of men's interests, and the less ingenuous character of people's lives. These are the inevitable accompaniments of greatly increased population and of the grand developments of later years, when steam and electricity have made relationships with the colonies as intimate as those of the three kingdoms used to be.

Within doors the change is also marked. Time was when even in the largest bank offices in Edinburgh the pervading spirit was that almost of the family—the family, however, of that period when affection was combined with reverence in the younger members. Doubtless, we have to go back to the first half of the century for that state of matters; the change having set in ere the period with which we deal had commenced. But it has proceeded with accelerating speed. The great increase in volume of business, the widely spreading systems of branches and correspondence, and the greater intricacy and multiplicity of exceptional details which inevitably accompany the advancement of civilisation, have rendered impossible the simple, happy life of the past. With multiplied numbers and increased subdivisions, directness of touch is lost. Artificial regulations have to take the place of personal supervision. The organisation becomes more mechanical, with the danger that the mechanism may insensibly be trusted to instead of the supervision, although designed merely as the medium to facilitate the supervision. It is like outdoor manœuvres superintended through telescopes and by signals, where the direct interchanging touch of personality is lost.

But it is not only the spirit of the age that has modified the character of banking in Scotland; or it may be more accurate to say that one development of modern ideas has had a large share in that modification. The enterprise of the large joint stock banks in steadily pushing out their branch systems, gradually extinguished the local banks. This movement had been in progress long before the period with which we are specially dealing, but it was not till then that local banking became a matter of ancient history, and that its spirit died out. The local banks were the successors of the older private banks, and differed but slightly from them in their manner of conducting business. Occupying comparatively small tracts of country, even when they had branch offices, they knew and were known all round. Consequently, no reasonable application for banking accommodation met with a refusal, and rural trade had an amount of attention which is impossible under a system of national banking where each bank seeks to base its prosperity not on the fortunes of a county, but on those of the whole country. It is a well ascertained fact that it is usually easier to obtain a banking advance at a head office than at a branch. The rationale of this is simple. An agent is, from the nature of his relationship to his principals, not only more diffident, but he is necessarily so tightly bound down by rules, as also by the spectre of supervision, that he will hesitate even where he has no doubt. In this connection it is well to remember that the local agents are not managers. At a head office, on the other hand, transactions are conducted on a larger scale, small risks will sometimes be taken "to mix," as stockbrokers would say, with other securities, or to avoid the appearance of stinginess in the fostering of industry. Besides, men always criticise a piece of business much more severely when another man does it, than when they do it themselves.

This position is the necessary result of the adoption of the national system of banking in preference to local banking. Every well managed bank maintains a stringent control over its branches ; and the more numerous and widespread the offices the more imperative will be the regulations. Complaints are often made by traders that they do not get the accommodation to which they are entitled. Of course the limits of their demands are much wider than any banker would acknowledge the propriety of ; but, as we have seen, the grumble has a basis of truth. But, all things considered, it can hardly be doubted that, while local banking tends to confer greater advantages on the community, it does so at the expense of the banks. If credit is more readily given, the danger of loss becomes more acute. Besides, the ratio of expense is higher with small than with large businesses. At the same time the national system gives greater opportunity for establishing the banking system on a sound and powerful basis. Typical instances of failure illustrative of pernicious working on both systems are to be found in the Ayr Bank and the Edinburgh and Glasgow Bank. The former was a local bank devoting its energies to fostering the agriculture of a county, and ruining itself through excess of zeal. The latter was a comparatively large and widespread bank with an excellent connection which, with ordinary prudence, might have been a permanently prosperous concern. But it had two head offices, each of which acted as if it had full control of the resources of the bank. This want of central control occasioned it grave difficulties which were only allayed by amalgamation and the loss of all the capital.

But if the banker has changed, his customers have changed also. Not only were there, as we have seen, more direct relationships between the banker and his customers, but the character of the latter was more ingenuous. The spirit of the age with its mottoes, "Diamond cut diamond," and "Deil tak' the hindmost," has introduced a mercenary spirit which has destroyed the fine old class of merchant traders who, shrewd and well able to protect their own interests, yet never dreamt of sharp practice. Their competition was above board, uncontaminated by Yankee cuteness, and doubtful conduct was comparatively rare. Under present conditions, a banker requires to cultivate the faculty of suspicion to a much greater extent than formerly, to avoid being victimised.

In treating of the evolution of Scottish banking, it is instructive to go further back than the limits of the period under discussion. It is sometimes said that traces of banking in Scotland are met with before 1695; but this would appear to be a misapprehension. Of course there were money-lenders, and dealers in exchange, but of actual banking I have never seen any indication, nor has any one, so far as I am aware, produced any instance. The earliest bankers were semi-government functionaries —at all events they were actuated by the governmental tone. This arose from the circumstances of the case. Although not a Government institution, the Bank of Scotland was erected under the auspices of the Government as a public institution. Its duties were of a national and public character, while its emoluments were for private appropriation, just as in the case of any officer of the State. The case of the Royal Bank was essentially similar, and that of the British Linen differs from it only in so far as the initial efforts of that establishment were more directly connected with trade than with finance. This aspect of their constitutions was fully recognised, at least up to the period we treat of. The distinction between the "banks," and "banking companies," was absolute; and of course the private "bankers" were a class by themselves. The last named disappeared finally more than fifty years ago, and had practically decayed at a still earlier date; and the first named gradually dropped their superior tone in the excitement of modern rivalry.

This result is much to be regretted, for there is no doubt that the sense of public responsibility was a material element in steadying the management of the three old banks. Indeed, but for this higher tone, there is reason to fear that they might not so well have withstood the difficulties of the eighteenth century. But the energetic growth of the younger banking companies, which went to the public instead of expecting customers to come to them, proved too strong a rivalry to permit of the maintenance of the old-world dignity. With the decay of private banking, the old banks had, in some measure, lost access to the people; for the private bankers (with the exception of Sir William Forbes, who stood on a higher footing than most of the others, and, perhaps, one or two more) acted as the lions' providers. Thenceforth, instead of the governmental functionaries' tone giving the lead, it was the banking companies, as exponents of modern trade competition, that moulded the character of Scottish banking. How far this has been publicly beneficial is a matter on which opinions may differ. I incline to think, however, that in any case it was inevitable. That it has had injurious effects can hardly be doubted; but this is by no means inconsistent with national benefit. For the spirit of vicarious sacrifice, whether voluntary or involuntary, is perennially at work.

Whither this evolution is trending, it is hard to say. It may be, perchance, to the selection of a more highly developed organism through the survival of the fittest, although, in the period of transition, the qualities which may in the future shine forth, are but dimly visible. Or it may be but a renewed example of the over-development and weakness—producing over-refinement—which accompany the decline of mighty empires. But doctrines of the down-grade school have no honour in the countries to which they refer—they hurt susceptibilities, and, worse still, there is no money in them. In any case it is instructive to discuss in detail various aspects of the inner life of Scottish banking.

CHAPTER IX.

ARRANGEMENTS AND FUNCTIONS.

" Order is Heaven's first law."
—POPE.

IN continuing our inquiry into the moral and esoteric aspects of Scottish banking, it falls naturally to deal with the details of the internal working of the Scottish banks. But it is questionable if considerations of symmetry and completeness would have secured its presence, as British writers are so little introspective that they treat more generally of causes and effects, than enter into descriptions of the machinery by which results are attained. Fortunately, however, in such matters our French friends are more logical; and the present writer was reminded, at the close of a kindly and appreciative notice of his *History of Banking in Scotland* which appeared in *La Réforme Sociale* of Paris, from the graceful pen of the editor, M. Pierre des Essars, that the omission of such details was a matter of regret. Fully recognising the justice of this criticism, the present opportunity is secured for the insertion of a descriptive chapter. The British reader is, at the same time, warned that it is of a purely elementary character, and may be skipped without detriment to any knowledge he may desire to have of the purport of this volume.

Preliminary to the consideration of the functions of the banks, it may be well briefly to describe the arrangements usually found in a Scottish banking office. The establishment usually consists of a governor, a deputy governor, extraordinary directors and ordinary directors; with, as executive officers, a general manager and a secretary. The governors and extraordinary directors take practically no part in the administration, their functions being almost purely ornamental. The real power is vested in the ordinary directors, the others being only consulted when there exists any desire for a division of responsibility. The other public officers are an accountant, a cashier (at the head of the cash department), and tellers (cashiers). The public office, in addition to the cash department, is divided into departments such as the cheque office (for current accounts), bill office (discounts, etc.), correspondence office, accountant's office (for general book-keeping), besides which there are the branch (superintendence) department, and law and transfer department. The nomenclature of officers, and divisions of work assigned to each, vary somewhat in different banks—thus the chief officer of the Bank of Scotland is styled treasurer; of the Royal Bank of Scotland, cashier—but in the main there is similarity. Of course, in branch offices, arrangements are on a smaller scale, but the system of business is the same.

A description of the practice of banking in Scotland may best be pursued by following the items of the published balance sheets. First we deal with the liabilities to the proprietors. The capital is usually in stock transferable in any quantities; but some even of the large banks hold it divided into shares. In the case of the three old banks, in virtue of their incorporation, no liability attaches to the holding of their capital stocks, except that the Bank of Scotland stock is only paid up to the extent of 13s. 4d. in the £1, and consequently proprietors are liable for other 6s. 8d. per £1 of their holdings. The rest (an old term still retained by the older banks, signifying the remainder of assets after all provisions and appropriations' or reserve fund has always been made a strong point with the Scottish banks; and the British Linen Co. has lately achieved the feat of making its rest considerably larger than the capital. Other liabilities to proprietors consist of profit balances appropriated to dividend purposes, or carried forward as a nest-egg to the next year.

Turning to the public liabilities, the most important department of a bank's business, so far as extent of *clientèle* is concerned, is connected with the deposit business. It is of two classes: creditor balances of current accounts, and sums lodged on deposit receipt. In both cases the money is held by the bank repayable on demand. No interest is now allowed on current accounts. On deposit receipts interest runs at present at 1 per cent.*—the lowest rate ever recorded. To secure interest, however, the money must be undisturbed for at least thirty days. Money can be lodged or drawn at will, no notice being required in either case. By an unwritten understanding £10 is regarded as a minimum sum receivable; but there is no official restriction. The number of depositors, as given in the blue book of 1875, was 417,657, with an average deposit of about £182 10s. The large extent to which the banking system commends itself to the public is strikingly shown by these figures and by the fact that,

* Increased, 14th Oct., to 1¼ per cent.

including all ages and conditions of the people, fully one-eighth of the population were, twenty years ago, customers of one or other of the banks. Doubtless there is some over-lapping—one person having deposits with more than one bank—but there is little reason to suppose that this element would materially affect the proportion. Of the total deposits, according to the experience of five of the banks, 75 per cent. were held on deposit receipts, and 25 per cent. on current accounts. The proportion of deposit-receipt money is probably greater in the rural than in the urban district. It may be presumed that, since the date of the parliamentary inquiry, there has been a slight modification in these proportions, owing to the cessation of the allowance of interest on current accounts. A competent authority estimates the present proportions as 77 per cent. and 23 per cent. respectively.

It would be interesting to know how far the number of depositors, and the average amount of deposit, have grown during the same period. As the total deposits have increased by 19½ per cent., it might be expected that the depositors now number nearly 500,000; but as the population has grown at a less rapid rate, it is probable that the principal increase has been in the average amount of deposit.

The next item calling for attention is the note circulation. Although not now of the relative importance in a bank's economy that it used to be, the right of issue is still regarded as one of the vital privileges. While there was no restriction on issues, the function was a highly profitable and inexpensive department of the banking business; for, of course, the banks got the use of the money represented by their notes at no greater outlay than the cost of the manufacture of the documents, and the clerical expenses of issuing and retiring them. Even yet, when the restrictions now in force, combined with the largely extended over-issues necessitating the retention of a large stock of sovereigns, have practically abolished the direct profit on issuing, the privilege is of material benefit to the banks. This benefit they share with the public. As is well known the Scottish banks have established branches in numerous sparsely populated localities where no other banking system could survive. Of course the cause assigned is Scottish thrift. But even the careful Scot could never have accomplished the feat on the basis of a metallic till. It is because of their paper till-money that the banks are able to carry on these branches. So long as the notes are in the hands of the bank they represent no actual value; but they are very useful in so far as, by the simple action of passing over the counter, they at once assume all the functions of money. It is only then that the issuing bank is under the necessity of taking them into account in studying its reserve of gold coin. Moreover, the banks have the advantage of basing their gold reserve on their average circulation of each four weeks, and not on the actual issues. Their real circulations are often much greater than appears by the monthly statement published by the Government department (of which a specimen is subjoined). For a week of expanded circulation is only averaged, and the normal circulation is reduced to its lowest point at the end of each week. Owing to the active and systematic exchanges made by the issuing banks at the close of each week, the circulation is brought down to low-water mark for the returns to Government. These are made every four weeks; and the average of the four weeks' figures, less the amount of the so-called authorised issue, is the sum that must be shown to have been covered by gold coin at the head office or principal place of issue. It will be noticed that the Government statement shows the total amount of gold and silver coin in the hands of each bank, including the branches. Why this should be, is one of the riddles connected with Government supervision of the issues which bankers have for fifty years endeavoured unsuccessfully to solve. The coin at the branches does not count as cover for the notes. The denominations of notes issued are £1, £5, £10, £20, and £100. Owing to the natural desire not to increase un-

CIRCULATION OF SCOTTISH BANKS.

An account, pursuant to the Act 8 and 9 Vict., cap. 38, of the amount of bank notes authorised by law to be issued by the several banks of issue in Scotland, and the average amount of bank notes in circulation, and of coin held during the four weeks ending Saturday, 28th November, 1896.

Name and Title as set forth in Licence.	Circulation Authorised by Certificate.	Average Circulation during Four Weeks.	Average Amount of Coin held during Four Weeks.
Bank of Scotland	£343,418	£1,180,615	£1,041,724
Royal Bank of Scotland	216,451	1,006,470	964,665
British Linen Company	438,024	923,051	645,946
Commercial Bank of Scotland	374,880	1,009,352	772,735
National Bank of Scotland	297,024	896,243	761,263
Union Bank of Scotland	454,346	1,051,277	769,143
Town & County Banking Co.	70,133	328,889	301,410
North of Scotland Banking Co.	154,319	485,404	362,759
Clydesdale Banking Co.	274,321	788,036	638,677
Caledonian Banking Co.	53,434	158,702	124,570

necessarily their stock of gold, the banks endeavour to secure all retirable notes as soon as possible. For this purpose exchanges are made daily at every place throughout the country where two or more banks are represented, balances being settled by drafts on Edinburgh. Unexchangeable notes, *i.e.*, those of banks not locally represented, are sent by post to Edinburgh, and exchanged there.

The exchange at Edinburgh, which is the final note clearing for the whole country, is held daily in the Bankers' Exchange and Clearing House building, No. 23 St. Andrew Square (which is the joint property of the banks). A second exchange, for large notes only, is held on Saturdays at one o'clock so as to exhaust that day's collections. Settlements are conducted each alternate month by the Bank of Scotland and by the Royal Bank of Scotland, neither of which, however, has any responsibility in respect of the transactions. On Mondays and Thursdays, the balances are included in the general settlement of the exchange and clearing. On the other days of the week, unless a general settlement fall on any of those days, the exchange balances are combined with the general balance of the clearing of the same day. On Saturday afternoon the settling bank grants and receives vouchers for the balances, which are carried into the next day's clearing, and bear interest at deposit receipt rate. When the balances of the general settlement have been struck, the particulars are entered in a record provided for the purpose, and the banks which are debtors in the settlement send, on the same day, to the banks which are creditors, letters intimating that in four days thereafter the respective amounts due will be transferred to their credit in London. At the same time the debtor banks pay interest on their balances for four days at 3 per cent. Failure duly to make the transfer entails immediate exclusion from the exchange and clearing. Where exchanges are established in provincial towns, the exchangeable notes received at the local agencies must be exchanged there, and not forwarded to meet exchanges in Edinburgh or elsewhere. The banks are mutually bound to bring all their exchangeable notes to the exchange rooms; and not to issue each other's notes without permission. Three months' notice of withdrawal from the agreement is required.

The remittance business is important more from the multiplicity of transactions than from its profitableness. Drafts (letters of credit), payable on demand, are drawn by any office of the bank on itself or any other office of the bank, on corresponding banks in places in Scotland where the drawing bank is not represented, on correspondents in England, Ireland and throughout the world. The charges are very moderate. Remittances between branches within the same locality—for example, between Edinburgh and Leith—cost only the Government 1d. stamp. Otherwise within Scotland the charge is 1s. per cent. with a minimum of 6d. (7d. including stamp, which is, of course, charged in all cases). The exchange with London is 1s. per cent., and with the provinces of England and Ireland 2s. 6d. per cent. Remittances may be made to London without cost by transfer deferring payment for ten days, or by the issue of a draft at fourteen days' date. Since 15th March last, drafts on Scotland and London, for sums not exceeding £5, are issued at 3d., and from £5 to £10 at 4d. Circular notes and special letters of credit for travellers abroad are also issued without cost to customers. There are numerous other remittance arrangements of a similarly reasonable character which need not be detailed here.

The only other item among the liabilities to be considered is the acceptances. This department of business arises from the superior credit attaching to the obligation of a banking house. Merchants therefore frequently request their bankers to accept bills which have been drawn on them, which, on suitable provision for meeting the acceptance when due, the bankers undertake to do as a regular matter of business. In consequence of their acceptance, the bill becomes what is styled "bank paper," and is negotiable and discountable on much more favourable terms than had it remained a merchant's acceptance. Marginal bills issued to travellers authorising them to draw for any sums within a fixed maximum are also included in this category. These bills, or letters of credit, being presented to a banker, he marks the amount and date of payment of such sum as may be drawn through him. But probably the largest item among the acceptances is occasioned by the drafts of foreign and colonial banks accepted by the London offices of the banks for purely remittance purposes. The acceptances are often classed with the drafts, as partaking with them of the character of remittance business; but they have sufficient individuality to be treated as a special item in bankers' balance sheets. Indeed, by not a few, this department of business is regarded as one attended by risks of a specially hazardous description.

We have now to treat of the other side of the bank's balance sheets, *viz.*, the assets. The first item claiming attention is a composite one—the banking advances. Unfortunately some of the banks do not give the amount of their discounts separately, and some even group all the advances in one sum. But for practical purposes it is necessary to divide the advances into three groups. (*a*) The bills discounted either are, or are desired to be, the largest of these sections. This is, so to speak, the most "bankingest" of all a bank's business. But there are bills and bills, from the bank paper we have already referred to and the finest mercantile acceptances, to the trumpery promissory note of the struggling trader, or the wind bill of the man about town. The highest class of paper is, of course, taken at special rates. Floating balances are largely placed thus in the London market, when opportunity offers; but even locally special lines of discount are arranged in particular cases. But between the two extremes we have mentioned, there is a grand field in which the expert banker can reap a good harvest without an undue quantity of tares. No doubt the cash payment system which has grown so much in recent years tends to displace this class of paper; but even yet there are many shrewd and honest traders without much capital who, when encouraged, bring good business to a bank in the process of building up their own fortunes. For ordinary discount purposes, bills are grouped as London and "other," of three months, four months and upward currencies. When the money market is particularly weak it is customary to introduce a two months' rate. London bills are usually charged $\frac{1}{2}$ per cent. less than other; and each grade of currency differs by $\frac{1}{2}$ per cent. These terms are for mercantile paper; other acceptances being charged higher rates.

(b) Advances on current accounts form another important class. They are divisible into (1) cash accounts, (2) other secured overdrafts, and (3) unsecured overdrafts. (1) The cash account, or cash credit, is based on an agreement with the bank, embodied in a formal bond, between three or more parties, that the drafts of one of them (styled the drawer), in account current, are guaranteed to a maximum amount on balance, with interest accrued. The parties are jointly and severally liable for the whole debt, including other obligations up to the amount of the credit, and the bank is entitled to withdraw the credit and call up the debt at any time. At one time, but not within the period we are dealing with, a commission, in addition to interest, was charged on the cash accounts, but the practice does not seem to have been long continued. Within the amount of the authorised credit, lodgments and drawings may be made at will, interest being only charged on the debtor balance at the close of each day's transactions. It is an excellent system, especially for a poor country, as Scotland used to be. But great accumulations of capital, and the low price of money, make it now an unduly expensive method of getting accommodation. It was at its best during the period of free issues, when, as an ally of the notes, and as a means of extending their circulation, it was a great source of profit to the banks. But the day of the cash account is practically done. (2) Overdrafts of accounts are also permitted against specific securities, such as holdings of the capital stock of the bank itself; stocks, shares and bonds of other approved companies or public bodies transferred to the bank; letters of guarantee by substantial securities; policies of life assurance within surrender value, or with special provision for payment of premiums; bonded warehouse warrants, etc. Advances to holders of bank stock are particularly simple on account of a usual provision of lien on the part of the banks over the stock of proprietors indebted to them. This facility used to be held out as a special inducement by promoters of new banks to intending subscribers for shares. (3) Unsecured overdrafts are quite irregular, and are distinctly discouraged. At the same time it is practically impossible to avoid them. It is a simple matter to return Bill Bounder's cheque; but a prudent banker will not offend his esteemed customers, or cast a slight on their credit, for the risk implied in making an advance to them without pre-arrangement. It is, however, always expected that authority to overdraw be obtained beforehand; indeed, even courtesy would imply that this be done. This is one of the departments in which the expert banker shines. He knows when quietly to say "No," and when, without a moment's hesitation, to say "Delighted, my dear sir, to give you any accommodation". The amateur banker hesitates in both cases, with the result that Bill Bounder thinks he may try again, while Sandy Soundman feels that what he intended as business is regarded as a favour conferred.

(c) The third group of advances to be considered is the loans on Stock Exchange and other special securities. Although this is now an extensively cultivated branch of the banks' business, it was not one originally devised by them. On the contrary, its earliest practitioners were vigorously denounced by the orthodox bankers of their day. This class of business originated with the Exchange Banks, themselves a product of the railway mania time, and of which the late Duncan McLaren, a distinguished citizen of Edinburgh (subsequently M.P.), and George Kinnear (one of an Edinburgh banker's family), in Glasgow, were energetic pioneers. The crisis of 1848 proved, however, too much for them in their immature experience. All but one, which still carries on a sort of galvanised existence, have been swept away, and the banks proper now reap where they sowed. The system has, however, been modified, the rash and hap-hazard all-trusting frame of mind having been discarded. The practice now is that marketable securities are made over to the bank against an inoperative advance of say four-fifths of the market value for a fixed period (say three months).

At the end of the fixed period the loan must be repaid, unless a renewal be agreed on. This implies a revaluation of the securities and a reconsideration of rates of interest. The minimum rates, except in special cases, are the same as those for Scotch bills.

(d) Advances are also made in exceptional cases on heritable (or real estate) bonds. But from the essential principles of banking business this department is always restricted to a small proportion of the total advances, the liquidity of which is a matter of primary importance never lost sight of.

The next item among the assets, customers' liabilities for acceptances and indorsements, is of the nature of banking advances, although it does not involve absolute advances until the maturity of the acceptances; and in cases where the money has been lodged, or where cash is paid at the due date, no advance occurs. Still there is always the liability to make an advance, except in the few cases of predeposit.

The heritable property, or real estate, of the banks is an item of much importance. But it hardly comes within the category of subjects pertaining to practical banking. Besides, it has been treated of at some length in the first part of this book. It may, however, be remarked, that it is usual to divide the property into two or three classes: (1) Bank buildings at head office and branches from which, of course, no direct return is obtained. (2) Bank property in London, if any. All the Edinburgh and Glasgow banks have offices in London, and in almost every case the building is the freehold property of the bank. As a rule, a considerable portion of the London offices is let to other companies or firms. And

(3) heritable property yielding rent. From various causes, but chiefly in the realisation of bad debts, houses, business premises and land come into the bank's possession. Of course, the possession is meant to be only temporary, but, as some is sold, other falls in, and, in any case, such property is not at all times saleable at an acceptable price.

Reference has already been made to the Clearing House in its relationship to its little, but older, sister, the Exchange; but it will be necessary to devote special attention to it. Although there are comparatively few towns in which an organised Clearing House has been established, facilities exist all over the country for the expeditious retirement of cheques by direct presentation by post, and the return of " debit vouchers " which are cleared in their place. The Edinburgh Clearing House is the final clearing, in which not only the local business is transacted, but the balances of clearings elsewhere, the " debit vouchers " just mentioned, and the balances of the note exchanges are included. The house is open every business day at one o'clock, except on Saturdays and local holidays, when it meets at eleven. Additional clearings are arranged for at the terms of Whitsunday and Martinmas when business is specially voluminous. Each representative of the banks is furnished with a set of books for the various banks (formed for writing in duplicate by means of impressive paper interleaved), in which the documents delivered by him are entered, summed, and tested before he goes to the Clearing House; and he hands to each of the other banks a duplicate list along with the documents delivered. He has also a book in which he strikes the balances. In addition to demand documents, bills domiciled at local banks, and documents payable elsewhere in Scotland where the Clearing Bank has not a branch or correspondent, may be passed through the Clearing House.

The two oldest banks undertake the settlement of the clearings of each alternate month. On Mondays and Thursdays the balances are included in the general settlement of the exchange and clearing. On other days the settling bank receives from those banks which are *debtors* on the clearing settlement (with which is included the balance of the exchange) and gives to those which are *creditors*, exchange vouchers for the respective balances, within one hour after the striking of the clearing balances. These vouchers are brought into the next clearing, and bear interest from the date of issue till the date of that clearing, at the deposit receipt rate current on the day of settlement. The interest is included in the voucher given for the balance. Of course, the banks undertaking the settlement of the clearings incur no responsibility whatever in respect of these transactions; and all expenses connected with the Clearing House are borne by the banks in equal proportions. The presently existing rules are dated 25th May, 1888.

The branches of the Scottish banks are agencies pure and simple; not partaking of the nature of branch banks, such as are to be found in England and elsewhere. The agent is merely the hand of the head office, put out or drawn back as directed. This system tends to preserve soundness in the business; but it curtails it, and dwarfs the banking experience of the staffs. Of course in the large towns the agents require to have a little more latitude; but they are apt to find that with more latitude they may get out of their bearings and be required to make their own reckoning. A Scottish agent usually finds that his best plan is to keep within the letter of his instructions, and never to take personal responsibilities. The business of the bank may be stunted in the locality; but the head office will have all the more money to finance with; and the agent acquires a reputation for careful management. This state of matters is a constant source of discontent among traders in the provinces; but any material alteration of it is improbable. It is the inevitable result of the centralising process which has been in operation for many years past. Almost all local banking vitality has been eliminated; and the small remnant will probably be obliterated ere long.

From our sketch of the functions of the banks, it will be seen that banking in Scotland is similar to banking elsewhere. When allusion is made to the peculiarities or specialties of the system, little more is meant than that particular conditions have slightly modified general banking arrangements. Perhaps the most distinguishing, and undoubtedly the most lauded, of Scottish banking practices, is the cash account. And yet, after all, what more is it than an advance under collateral guarantee? The mind is apt to be dazzled by terms. If the system had been styled "joint guarantee credits" no one would have seen anything extraordinary in it. While saying this we do not, however, mean to ignore the great work achieved under its operations. But it was not any ingenuity of system, but simply the fact that shrewd bankers made advances to well selected traders, that secured success. In a word, it was the conditions then existing both as regards men and business, not any peculiarity of machinery, that should be studied. The same work would be impossible now—even the type of banker is not now cultivated. Indeed the Scottish field is but a poor training school. No doubt successful bankers from all quarters of the habitable (and unhabitable) globe hail from Scotland. But it was as clerks they left their native land; they learned to be bankers elsewhere. The Scottish banks are good nurseries of the raw material; but they do not manufacture bankers in any considerable quantity.

CHAPTER X.

BANK AGENTS.*

" He who is more elevated by the distinction of an honourable appointment, than oppressed by a sense of its obligations, is not likely to improve either himself or others."—PROFESSOR W. B. HODGSON.

THE position of a bank agent, or local manager, is one of very considerable importance. In Scotland he is a better known member of society than in England, as the total absence of private bankers and small joint-stock banks, together with the extended systems of branches of large establishments, devolves upon him in great measure the position of the banker strictly so called. Strictly speaking, a banker is one who, having funds of his own employed in banking business, does himself take an active part in managing the business. Many bank officers are holders of stock of the banks with which they are connected, and might thus seem to come within the above definition; but, in as far as their connection with the banks is not in virtue of their share in the capital, but by reason of office specially conferred on them for specific remuneration, it is evident that they are not thus entitled to the designation. In point of fact, only members of private banking firms can be properly called bankers. But as in Scotland there are no private bankers,

* *Scottish Banking and Insurance Magazine*, Dec., 1880.

and as it would be an absurdity to say that there are no bankers, it is usual to consider all bank officers who are endowed with official powers as bankers. In this category, then, will be included general managers, secretaries, local managers or agents, and all other officers who have the right to sign in name of the companies whose business they are conducting. In this sense bank agents form the largest proportion of the body of bankers in Scotland, for, while there are about 1000 of them, there are only about fifty other bank officials.

It is not, however, from their number alone, or chiefly, that they are particularly deserving of attention. Although they are subordinates, acting under the supervision of their head offices, they have scope for a large amount of independent judgment and action; and they hold an influential position in their respective districts, as among the most important members of the business and professional classes of the community. A head office will not interfere much with an efficient agent, but will rather be prejudiced in favour of his representations. But if he exhibits deficiency of judgment, or want of business habit, his returns and reports regarding the business of his office will be subjected to specially minute inspection, and his liberty of action will be circumscribed. It is in the matter of business habits, and technical knowledge of banking, that agents are usually most deficient. Self-preservation makes them cautious in giving advances. Indeed, applicants for accommodation, especially when the amount involved is considerable, sometimes find head offices, or private bankers, more ready to entertain their proposals than branch offices. This is not, however, so much owing to the action of agents, as to the fact that principals are naturally more diffident in matters brought before them through the medium of representatives, than they are in direct communications. This fact is often adduced as an argument against the branch system of banking as compared with a multiplicity of banks. But it must be recollected that the former principle has the advantage in the all-important elements of solidity and the economy of capital. As regards technical and business knowledge, bank agents in this country are probably behind their brethren of England, and even of Ireland. In these countries, but especially in England, the practice of appointing outsiders to the more important offices in banks is much rarer than in Scotland. The typical Scotch bank agent is one who, successful as a country lawyer, or perhaps active and intelligent as a provincial shopkeeper, or influential as a rural residenter of means, has sought to employ the comparative leisure he has attained to, in the light and respectable, if not over remunerative, work of superintending a village bank office. It is not expected that he should be well versed in the technicalities of his new occupation. If he can show a good balance of deposits he is considered a success. And he usually does so, unless, as sometimes happens, there is not much floating capital in the district; or over competition has produced an insufficient average among several rival banks.

Now, laying aside the question of local influence *versus* technical knowledge, as a matter of policy in bank management, it does seem advisable that the representatives of the various banks throughout the country, and at sub-offices in the large towns, should be thoroughly acquainted with the leading points pertaining to the theory and practice of banking. The system of branch office management pursued in Scotland makes this of comparatively small importance as far as the banks themselves are concerned ; but, in his intercourse with his customers and friends, many a bank agent must feel that, beyond the ordinary routine of his office, he is somewhat deficient in sustaining the character of a banker. It is true that in this respect he is no worse than many other bank officers ; but they will not readily rise to official rank unless they set themselves to show more aptitude for their business, while he is placed in a position from which the public, if not his directors, expect special knowledge. Agents, as a rule, have a good deal of spare time which they might advantageously occupy in the study of banking, currency, and general finance. There is a popular idea that these are dismal subjects ; but, if they are not so absorbing as science, philosophy, and art, they are full of interest to those who study them aright, and especially so to those who have the opportunity of practical contact with their operations.

Besides country agents, to whom we have been specially referring, there are the agents or district managers in the large towns. These, as a rule, are practical bankers who, although subject to supervision, have, on their own responsibility, to carry on from hour to hour large transactions without previous reference to their head offices. This is a necessary consequence of the nature and magnitude of the business of a great centre of commerce. Thus the offices of the Edinburgh banks in Glasgow are, as far as the public is concerned, independent banks. The principal branch offices in Dundee, Aberdeen, and elsewhere, are similarly circumstanced. It might be well if, in such cases, the chief local officer were more generally designated "manager," as the term "agent" implies more limited powers than are accorded to the banks' representatives in such large cities. The tendency lately shown to confer the title "general manager" on the principal officer of a bank in its corporate capacity seems to point in this direction.

An important question in connection with the duties of bank agents is the propriety of canvassing for deposits. Deposited money is the life-blood of banks, and to its preservation and increase the efforts of agents are mainly devoted. It may be advisable in some cases to cultivate the custom of a good borrower, but, as a general rule, a bank has no difficulty in lending out its funds. It is true that money does at times accumulate inconveniently in a banker's hands, but over a series of years the money market adjusts itself, and even when he has more deposits than he actually requires for his business, a banker will not willingly part with his deposit customers. But while the prosperity of a bank depends, apart from management, on the amount of its deposits, it by no means follows that the attainment of that end will justify all efforts for its accomplishment. A high tone of banking morality will not sanction systematic canvassing for business. A banker degrades his profession by such action. The public should be his clients, not he theirs. A commercial traveller does not demean himself by canvassing for custom, because that is the legitimate object of his work in life, and because his dealings are with men whose business it is to have as much knowledge of his wares as he has himself. But, were he to call at private houses and solicit orders, he would become a pedlar, and would thus fall in the social scale. Similarly, a banker who asks people to transfer their accounts from another bank to his, places both himself and the institution he represents in a position inconsistent with the independence of a banker, and unworthy of a great establishment. There is a great difference in this respect, although it is not always perceived, between banks and insurance companies; for it is one thing for an insurance agent to endeavour to secure a specific transaction which might be carried through in a thousand different ways, all requiring explanation to be understood by most persons, and an altogether different thing for a bank agent to seek surreptitiously to undermine a continuous business relationship, such as exists between a banker and his customers, without any show of advantage to the person solicited. A bank agent should *attract* business; he should not require to *solicit* it.

But, while it is inexpedient for a banker to hunt for business, it does not follow that he is to sit passively in his chair waiting for customers, like a spider for flies. The most successful agents are those who are well known as active, practical business men. Tennyson's "Northern Farmer's" advice to his son was, "Doänt thou marry for münny, but goä wheer münny is". Without entering on an examination of this dictum as a point in casuistry, it may be held as a fact, that bank agents who are moving among the moneyed people of their districts, and who are best known and respected by the well-to-do of all classes, are much more successful in the long run than those who go about hat in hand to pick up the small deposits of persons whose transactions are not sufficiently important to make it a matter of difficulty to leave their banker. Nominally all the banks discourage canvassing; and, although one or two of them have more or less indulged in it, it is not regarded as good form.

But a banker should be a "known" man. He should be seen at "kirk and market," as the saying is; his name should appear in connection with religious and philanthropic objects, he should not hide his light under a bushel; and while he need not bother people like an "up-to-date take-your-life" insurance canvasser, he should mix freely and continuously with other men. Social functions should be his natural habitat, and if he have the gift of speech or other accomplishment, it is well that it should be in evidence. Unknown bankers may be as wise as Solomon, but they will do little towards extending their business compared with their brainless rivals who are known to every one.

CHAPTER XI.

BANK OFFICERS.*

" Very few live by choice: every man is placed in his present condition by causes which acted without his foresight, and with which he did not always willingly co-operate."—JOHNSON in *Rasselas*.

IN its business aspects, banking in Scotland has been brought to a point of perfection which has called forth the commendation of economists in all nations. But it is to be feared that the energies of Scottish bankers have been so exclusively devoted to the work in hand, as to leave very little leisure for theoretic study, and almost entirely to divert attention from the question of the well-being of the *personnel* of the profession. So stagnant has been the condition of Scottish bank clerks, that in Scotland banking is popularly regarded as the most dismal and hopeless of respectable professions. A Scottish bank clerk vegetates—there is life in him, possibilities, latent faculties, but the almost invariable practice is to leave these dormant as long as possible. Training, in the sense of gradually educating the embryo banker for business responsibilities, is virtually non-existent in bank offices. Valuable work in this direction is now being carried on by the Institute of Bankers, but it is essential that, in addition to general and theoretic knowledge, experience

* *Scottish Banking and Insurance Magazine*, Oct., 1879.

should be acquired in practice. But in the majority of Scottish banks the young men are not only left to pick up their knowledge as they best may, but every generous impulse, laudable ambition, or inducement to activity and interest is chilled, if not annihilated, by the comparative inattention to which their special interests are subjected.

That this matter has, in one shape or another, repeatedly been considered by directors and managers is unquestionable. What we object to is, that no permanent solution of the question has been seriously sought for. Whenever it comes up it is settled by some temporary measure. An all-round bonus, a general increase of salaries, or a few special promotions, are the expedients with which murmurs are suppressed for the time being. Many will say, and actually do say, "What more can be done? Banking at best is but a slow and monotonous business in which prizes are few and difficult of attainment. Besides, most of the work is of such a nature that it does not merit great remuneration." This is the position usually taken up by *laissez faire* bank philosophers, and they think that nothing further can be said on the subject. For our part, we agree with their premises, but we demur to their deductions. We believe that banking is a monotonous and slow business, without many inducements to energy or opportunities for ability, seeing it has been systematically made so; and we do not doubt that, for the most part, clerks' salaries are in accordance with the nature of their employment.

The root of all the nerveless languor, hopeless discontent, and spasmodic dissatisfaction so often displayed by bank clerks is to be found in the absence of promotion.

The Psalmist's words, that "promotion cometh neither from the east, nor from the west, nor from the south," are literally exemplified in the case of Scottish bank clerks, although, doubtless, they were not designed for such an application. The majority of good appointments in banking establishments in Scotland (in England and Ireland the conditions are reversed) were, until lately, conferred on outsiders. This practice was brought about, innocently enough, by the manner in which the banking system was developed. When branches were being struck out, exterior influence was generally necessary to the formation of a business connection. But it by no means follows that, where that end has been attained, a continuance of the system is advisable. Indeed, it is demonstrable that, by the perpetuation of the practice, the banks are themselves losers. While they were supporting a large array of country lawyers and tradesmen for the sake of their "countenance" (the work being done by bred bankers in a subordinate capacity), they were yearly accumulating in their service, at slowly increasing salaries, large bodies of men who, qualified by years of service, would gladly have undertaken both the responsibilities and the duties for the same remuneration as is paid to the agents, and leave their clerical duties to be performed by younger men at smaller salaries. This would result in a sensible reduction in salary expenditure at the larger offices. But not only so. Branch work would be cheaper and better done, as, with professional agents, extra assistance might to some extent be dispensed with.

Some agents may feel aggrieved by these remarks, but we would submit the following considerations to their unbiased judgment. Natural shrewdness and business-like qualities, combined with prolonged banking experience, doubtless enable most of them to fulfil their duties in a satisfactory manner; but what were their initial experiences? For it is in regard to new appointments only that we are referring. Did they not feel very much out of their element in taking charge of an entirely new kind of business? Moreover, would they consider it a safe or judicious proceeding to entrust their respective businesses (in which, presumably, they served long and laborious apprenticeship) to the direction of men bred to other trades? Without doubt they would condemn such an action as unwise, and, if done to their prejudice, as unjust. The point of view of the old unpromoted bank officer is analogous. *Ne sutor ultra crepidam.*

It is not specially, however, in regard to agencies that our remarks apply, but to the system, or rather want of system, which prevails in connection with the advancement of young bankers. From the time of their entrance into the service they should have reason to feel that they are in a current of promotion, from the benefits of which only their own incompetency can exclude them. A heartfelt *esprit de corps* should be carefully encouraged in each establishment. This, however, can only be accomplished by making the staff happy in their present circumstances and hopeful of their future prospects. It is but poor service whose spirit is found only in pay. If higher and more generous feelings are not brought actively into play, there must be some radical defect either in the men themselves or in the arrangements to which they are subjected. And this brings us to another point. We have hitherto spoken mostly on behalf of the junior officers, but we do not desire to delude them into the belief that they are ill-used. We believe that more beneficial arrangements might be made for their advancement, but on the other hand, it cannot be doubted they have much to be thankful for. A bank clerk's circumstances will contrast very favourably with those of any other description of clerk, with, perhaps, the exception of the Government service. The one point in which he is unfavourably placed, is the difficulty he experiences in rising to a higher position. Lawyers' and merchants' clerks, while not as a rule in as easy circumstances, have much wider possibilities open to them. It is this that has induced us to bring forward their claims at the present time, and to seek to preserve to them, if not a practical monopoly, yet a large share of the opportunities which legitimately offer in their own profession. Let them not forget, however, that much lies in their own power towards the attainment of this end, in earnestly striving to qualify themselves for official responsibilities, by diligent study of all matters connected with the history, theory, and practice of banking. In this they will as truly be fulfilling their duty to themselves as to their employers.

In the opinion of many the discussion of this subject may not seem germane to the public view of business affairs, but should be left entirely to the realm of private adjustment. If, however, it be remembered that the success of business depends not alone on the few minds and bodies who have the direction of it, but to a large extent on the combined and mutually aiding efforts of all who are engaged in it, it will be seen that the condition of banking staffs is a very important one both for the proprietors and for the public. As well might it be said that a government need only appoint a general and give him a sufficient number of soldiers, counted by head, irrespective of quality or of physical or moral conditions, wherewith to conduct a campaign. A bank staff should be carefully and considerately graded from the top to the bottom, infused with loyalty and *esprit de corps*, filled with enthusiasm, and insensibly convinced that conjoint devotion to the interests of their establishment is consonant with their lifelong welfare. Such a condition is easy of attainment, It does not mean extravagant pay or little work. It means the truest economy, and the most successful business results. But it involves some sacrifice on the part of superiors to consideration of their personal relationships to their subordinates.

CHAPTER XII.

STAFF ASPECTS AND THE INSTITUTE.*

> "The constant service of the antique world,
> When service sweat for duty, not for meed!
> Thou art not for the fashion of these times,
> Where none will sweat but for promotion."
> —*As You Like It.*

To the young mind—to the mind so long as it retains its youthful freshness—advancement in business and social position is a matter of primary importance. And yet, in the seething multitude who are ever pressing forward, the fortunate form a very small minority. The great majority meet with disappointment after disappointment, and either learn the truth of Bacon's reflections on "Great Place," and accept their lot with Christian cheerfulness, or drift into chronic and unprofitable discontent. "It is a strange desire," says the philosopher, "to seeke Power and to lose liberty; or to seeke Power over others and to lose Power over a Man's Selfe." For the lowly place is unquestionably the most truly independent condition. But the desire to rise in the world is inborn, and, when pursued in a right spirit, is unquestionably laudable. Some must rule over others, and to leave the higher offices to the accidents of birth, or of chance, or of caprice, would be injurious to the common interest. Thus the desire for advancement is not

---

* *Scottish Banking and Insurance Magazine,* June, 1882; June, 1894; Dec., 1894.

only a matter of justifiable self-interest, but is even a public duty.

It cannot, however, be said that the most successful men are, as a rule, the most worthy. The theory that the most able men naturally rise to the surface does not by any means hold good throughout. Genius, indeed, when of a very high order, will undoubtedly assert itself; but with ordinary humanity, many potent factors of questionable character, which can only be overborne by the greatest minds, generally rule the earthly career of mortals. Of these self-assertion is one of the most powerful. The world takes most men at their own estimate. If one has no doubt of his own abilities, if he persistently presses his claims, and ruthlessly elbows others aside, he is pretty sure to secure recognition. Most men are too indolent or too blind to seek for or to see the talent that will not vulgarly assert itself—the "gem of purest ray serene, the dark unfathomed caves of ocean bear". The village Hampden, the mute inglorious Milton, the Cromwell guiltless of his country's blood, are left now, as in Thomas Gray's time, "to waste their sweetness on the desert air". Influence also exerts a baneful power against which merit hopelessly exhausts itself. The chance of being born a relative of a man in power, or having become allied to him by marriage, will prevail in the case of the most meagre intellect, when knowledge, experience, and every other true qualification are persistently unsuccessful. Another royal road to favour is persevering, unwavering toadyism. In some respects this is the most certain method of all, as it is the most ignoble. Few men, if any, can resist the subtle flatterer, who weaves his meshes full in the view of his victim. "Surely in vain the net is spread in the sight of any bird," says Solomon;

but the modern capacity for assimilating flattery is extensive. The man who will "stoop to conquer" by low arts is almost certain of success. Let him sing psalms with the pious, consort with the sinner, gossip with the scandal-monger, hang about the great man's son's club doors to run his errands, devote himself to church work, and conscientiously secure his future worldly interests by sacrificing his present nobility and virtue, and fortune will pour her favours on him.

Hypocrisy is an old and generally admitted method. So well, indeed, is it known, that the dissembler must now assume the mask of "*unaffected* piety," and this course is most successful when used as an accessory of other arts. As, however, it requires a large amount of dexterity, and inconvenient self-restraint, its votaries are not, perhaps, quite so numerous as its successfulness would warrant. It is still, however, much cultivated, mostly in an off-and-on kind of way. It prevails generally with the best people, and is least successful with the worldly, although the latter are prone enough to avail themselves of the services of those who seem to be religious. It is extraordinary how slow the world is to recognise the fact that the true saint (and there are many true saints in the world) does not flaunt his religion in the faces of others, but lets it speak through the medium of his walk and conversation.

The *rôle* of the importunate widow is also highly successful. Indeed the "poor mouth" generally is a great institution, and wonderfully helpful in a life career. It does not secure long steps, but the multiplicity of small ones it gathers in are quite as good. Moreover, there is no need to discontinue the practice with advancing prosperity, you can always be poorer than some other people.

Many a poor fellow, too proud to complain, or to sacrifice his conscientious independence, is distanced in the race for promotion by the whining of others actually less onerously weighted than himself. It is a curious fact, moreover, that this meanness hardly ever fails, for although some people pay no attention to its devotees, there are always some weak enough to be taken in.

Many persons, guiltless themselves of such mean actions, and too unsuspicious to perceive them in others, will deem this picture overdrawn. But it is not so. We are no misanthrope. We believe that there is much true earnestness and righteous purpose in the world—that many men, while they strive to rise, have no desire to do so by trampling on the rights of others, or by supplanting through invidious courses. But we speak what we have seen and known, and it is simply in accordance with the recorded experience of past centuries. Wickedness does triumph in the world now as it has done in the past. Its methods change, and, with advancing civilisation, it assumes more subtle phases; but its power is ever present.

The ingenuous youth must not, however, give way to despair when he contemplates the many chances against him in the battle of life. Good and earnest work, true purpose and steady perseverance will always greatly benefit him. He may see himself distanced by men who prefer by-ways and short cuts to the King's Highway; but he will secure the approbation of those whose opinion is of most value, and he will ever have a noble consciousness of honourable action. The price some men pay for their good fortune is infinitely extravagant. They debase their minds, expose themselves to continual humiliation, and sacrifice the highest pleasures of life for a reward which never satisfies them. For their greed is insatiable, and the more they get the more they grasp at. The longer and more honourable road is the more satisfactory. He who walks in it need never be unhappy, although he may never reach the goal. But it is quite permissible that he should learn from his rival the wisdom of the serpent, provided he retain the harmlessness of the dove. He should avail himself of every honourable means of advancing his interests. Many men let opportunities slip for want of energy or boldness in advancing their claims. The study of character is a great aid. Men in position like, as a rule, to be asked for their patronage, although some, the stronger-minded, are indifferent on the matter. Applications for situations or advancement seldom do the applicant any harm, and they often do him good indirectly, even when they fail in their immediate object. Importunity is often successful where the highest qualifications are ignored. Knowledge of the ways of the world is of great importance, and does not imply concurrence with them. A wise head and a sound heart are the best securities for a happy business career.

One of the most difficult, as it is one of the most important, duties connected with the management of a bank, is the selection of representatives and heads of departments. To its due fulfilment would be needed intuitive perception and knowledge of human nature in an exceptional degree. There are hardly any qualities, however, in regard to which people more frequently deceive themselves; so much so that they usually consider judgment of others as a matter of great simplicity. For similar reasons, the matter of appointments is not usually deemed a serious one, but rather as an opportunity for indulging in the pleasure of patronage. Any one who has taken the trouble to study the subject must be well aware of the palpable mistakes perpetually being made in the matter of appointments under one *régime*, and the infrequency and comparative unimportance of errors under another. But there is a further and a surer test. It will often be noticed that one establishment is, over a series of years, stationary or retrograding, while its neighbours, or some of them, are expanding in a more or less satisfactory manner. The remark is then frequently made of the one that it must be very energetically managed, and of the other that it seems to have gone to sleep. Energy in business is, no doubt, a valuable and powerful quality; but judiciousness and correct policy are much more important; and in all probability the remark is not accurate; the real reason of the difference being that, in the one case, the management has a thorough knowledge of human nature.

No one is more liable to be imposed on than the manager of a large establishment. It is utterly impossible that he can know those by whom he is surrounded throughout the extended system, of which he is the centre, unless he have not only that intuitive perception to which we have referred, but have or make the opportunity of testing the spirits as they pass before him. Some find it easiest to regard all men as alike, unless they show themselves to be different, and play them as the pieces on a draught-board. Others see differences, and while the mass are mere pawns, delight to honour their selected rooks and knights who move in fixed steps which can be previously calculated on. As no two men are alike, and as none walks according to fixed steps, but only pretends for his own purposes to do so, it is obvious that such states of mind can only be productive of disappointment. But there is, perhaps worse still, the selector who prides himself on his ability to tell at a glance the man he has to deal with. To him, a man who looks him straight in the eyes and contradicts him is a man of power. One who quietly defers to his superior authority is a weak man with no individuality. One who sucks the brains of others, and retails their ideas and knowledge as his own, is an extraordinarily clever fellow. Rough manners and noise are signs of strength : and interest in matters outside the daily routine shows want of concentration of attention. A glib-tongued detractor of others is viewed as a wide-awake gentleman, with a decided turn for studying character; while he who would scorn to injure a colleague behind his back is only a respectable but unobservant man.

An important principle in this connection, but one which is too seldom attended to, is the early training of the young men who enter the services. Nominally, of course, it is recognised ; but the rule is really either a dead letter or its execution is placed in the hands of those who would themselves require rudimentary lessons in reading character. It often happens, too, that a man who might be an excellent selector of agricultural labourers proves but an indifferent judge of the qualities of an embryo bank officer. This is the sort of person who cannot distinguish a poetic from a mechanical genius, and who thinks he has done an excellent and philanthropic piece of work when he sets a Burns to gauge whisky. Agents are greatly to blame in this respect, more especially in past times, when they seldom knew much of banking business, and regarded their connection with it more as a convenient adjunct to their principal vocation than as a duty to be seriously attended to. But even yet the training a young man gets is somewhat capricious and accidental, the staff being allowed to grow up somewhat like Topsy. The round pegs are allowed to roll about indiscriminately until they topple into square holes, and the square pegs have their edges jarred by being rammed into round holes, adjustment being left to the chapter of accidents.

Sometimes a clique of underlings, by engineering a policy during a series of years, practically monopolise the appointments. This is easier accomplished than might be supposed, by means of a consistent policy of commendation on the one hand, and of detraction on the other. Those who are not members of the choice circle are treated in the manner so forcibly described by Pope. The clique—

> Damn with faint praise, assent with civil leer,
> And, without sneering, teach the rest to sneer.
> Willing to wound, and yet afraid to strike,
> Just hint a fault, and hesitate dislike.

Against such action the management is powerless, because ignorant of its existence. But, all the same, it has potent influences on an establishment's progress. When employés are taken at their own valuation, and advancement becomes a game at grab, business interests are apt to suffer.

The Bankers' Institute has, no doubt, been useful in improving matters. But the damage done during the last thirty or forty years of active branch extension cannot be rectified except by lapse of time, even if the best endeavours were being made. Besides, there are many points of a banker's education which cannot be learned outside the office or tested in an examination room. And yet in many offices there is no one to teach them either by example or precept. Again, the young men are not accustomed to responsibility, or to look forward to undertaking it. This is partly owing to, and partly the cause of, a steady deterioration in the tone of the staffs since the last generation. This, of course, will be thought rank heresy, but, like much heresy, it is truth all the same. Indeed, unless a stop be put to the process, the next generation may witness serious results from it. One cause of this deterioration, but by no means the only one, is the great drain of the best young banking blood of Scotland to India and the colonies, which was so strongly developed during a prolonged period, which only ended with the recent collapse of Australasian banking.

It is but right, however, to say that a decided improvement has, thanks to the influence of the Bankers' Institute, taken place in regard to reserving the official appointments for men bred in the banks' own services, the neglect of which formerly has been the cause of woes unnumbered, which, however, there was no heavenly goddess to sing as in the days of Homer. A cure is not to be expected yet awhile; but, if the Institute will continue to hammer away for another generation, the second quarter of the twentieth century may be more favourable to bank officers than the last quarter of the nineteenth has been, and the banks be able to derive some benefit from higher mental qualities than are provided by a knowledge of the three Rs.

The Institute has now been long enough at work to permit a fair inquiry as to the utility of its existence. From the outset there have been many doubters. Even the students themselves often ask *cui bono?* To what purpose is all this labour? The young men look around them, and get but little encouragement from the survey of their surroundings, or from the contemplation of the result of the labours of those who have toiled before them. Thus they either gravitate into the vortex of disingenuousness at which they formerly shuddered; or ambition dies within them, as they sardonically think of the contrast between the dawn of hopes held out to them when their young hearts were fired with high ideals, and the sequel to their labours. And thus they ask, what is the good of the Institute?

We unhesitatingly answer, much every way. Not to speak of the pecuniary encouragements which the banks generously give to successful candidates, we would point out that every man who passes successfully through the Institute is an improved member of society, a man of higher culture than he was before. That of itself is a result which every generous mind must think a rich reward for all the labour undergone. But undoubtedly this would not alone be a sufficient *raison d'être* for an appurtenance of a practical profit-earning profession. Without entering on the relationship of the Institute of Bankers to the banks themselves, which is not our present subject, can it be fairly affirmed that it enables the members of the profession to achieve success in life? We undoubtingly say that it does. The mistake the young men make is when they enter on the course of study under the impression that success in the Institute will secure success in life. This it cannot do, and there is no reason why it should be expected to do so. Passing examinations is proof of knowledge, but is not a criterion of fitness for office, nor can it counteract the untoward conditions to which we have referred above. The Institute does not undertake to fight the battle of life for those who seek its aid; but it trains them for the fight, and places in their hands powerful weapons for attack and defence. The adverse conditions now existing have existed from the earliest times, although in our advanced civilisation and teeming population the struggle may be intensified. The Psalmist saw the wicked in great power, and spreading himself like a green bay tree, but he did not think that Providence was ill-using him thereby. The fact is that every one must fight for his own hand. Some choose ignoble means, which have in many ways great advantages over honourable and open methods. But the world is not so very wicked for all that. It is itself imposed upon, being really weak, short-sighted, and ignorant of human character. It seldom knows its best men, unless these either force themselves on its attention, or are shown to it by those wiser than the great majority; but, on the part of the bank authorities, there is a desire to do justly. In a crowded life struggle, however, the absolute recognition of every man's rights is a practical impossibility.

Though success in life is often achieved by ignoble means, such a course is not only contrary to ethical principle and repugnant to generous minds, but is not necessary to secure the desired result. Moreover, business cannot be conducted on philanthropic principles, and much of the result depends on each man's individual action. As Pistol says, "The world's mine oyster, which I with sword will open". So we would say to the Institute student, go forth with the weapons supplied to you, and with such other honourable accoutrements as are procurable, and attack the world. You will not find it so clever or strong but that any active-minded man, of full average ability and acquirements, can make his mark in it. But in all the fight maintain the highest tone. You are well entitled to use all the advantages you possess; you have the highest authority for being wise as serpents, but you must also be harmless as doves. As an old Earl of Shaftesbury says, quaintly but forcibly, "I would be virtuous for my own sake, though nobody were to know it, as I would be clean for my own sake, though nobody were to see me". And do not sit down and fret because a banking career is not for most an *El Dorado*, but be up and doing, and you will find that it has fair opportunities, and many substantial advantages, the attainment of which will depend, to a very great extent, on the conscientious and loyal observance of your own duties.

CHAPTER XIII.

COMPANY AUDITING.

"The value of testimony depends as much on the independence of the witness as on his competency."—ANON.

ONE of the prominent accompaniments of the crisis of 1878 was a vehement discussion on the subject of the independent auditing of accounts of banks, and as to the utility of the system as practised generally by joint-stock companies. What gave point to the discussion was, of course, the disclosures by the liquidators of the City of Glasgow Bank as to the state of the bank's affairs. With the single exception of the Bank of Scotland, which was in the habit of getting annually a certificate of "inspection" by two proprietors of stock, the banks in Scotland did not submit their accounts to the examination of any one outside their own services. In point of fact the question had never arisen, the banks having all been formed prior to the passing of the Companies Acts, when the practice of auditing became usual. Moreover, there was a belief that outside investigation of a bank's current business was inconsistent with that privacy which is requisite in dealing with customers' financial affairs. Incidentally it may be noticed that this is one of the points where the greater privacy of the system of private banking shows to advantage as contrasted with joint-stock banking. For the latter necessitates the extension of knowledge of the bank's affairs beyond those who are exclusively engaged in its work.

The practice of auditing is certainly not so applicable to banks as to general joint-stock companies, not only on account of the necessity for privacy, but also from the nature and extent of the transactions themselves. To be effective, an audit would require to be continuous and co-extensive with the bank's business, which, of course, is out of the question. Moreover, the more independent auditing is relied on, the less responsibility for the accuracy of the records is laid on directors. They naturally feel that, if the proprietors nominate and remunerate professional inspectors, it were a work of supererogation for them also to go minutely into details. But, whatever imperfections may attach to it, the practice of bank auditing has come to stay. If not so much of a safeguard as they imagine, it is a comfort to shareholders and creditors. As regards joint-stock companies in general, auditing is all-important. Yet it cannot be said that the regulations usually observed for carrying it out are by any means satisfactory. Yet, although the subject is of the utmost importance, its discussion does not appear to excite more than a moderate amount of attention. This is somewhat strange, when it is remembered how vast is the number of persons who are personally interested in the question, and how patently the defects of the system have of late been manifested. But shareholders are in some respects a surprisingly sheeplike body. They will complacently tumble into a ditch if their leader goes in. Their blind confidence in their directors is quite Christian in its character, and worthy of a better cause. One result of the discussion, however, was eminently satisfactory; no whisper of opposition was heard in answer to the general condemnation of the existing system. Indeed, it is quite apparent that only interested parties can uphold it, so unsatisfactory is it in principle and in its results.

Nominally, auditors are appointed by the shareholders, independently of the directors, to act as special guardians of their rights and interests, and to give the public reasonable confidence in the *bona fides* of the company. But how does this beautiful principle work out in practice? A shareholder is privately asked by one of the officials of the company to propose Mr. Protege, and another is asked to second the motion. Both being good-natured, or perhaps, expectant of future good, comply with a request, the declinature of which might be remembered disadvantageously on a subsequent occasion. The nominee enters upon his office with all the fervour of youth, and with the conscientious convictions of a Covenanter. Alas! he soon finds that youthful zeal cools in contact with official experience; and that convictions are very beautiful to look at, but too costly to wear. In a word, he discovers that he holds office at the will of the board, not of the shareholders.

Theoretically, auditors are chosen as disinterested and competent examiners of the companies' affairs. But in point of fact, they are always appointed for very different reasons. It may be safely asserted that not one election in a hundred turns either on the candidates' abilities or their moral principles. It is either a case of nepotism, or of one good turn deserving another. And there are always shareholders ready to advertise their claims for future remembrance, by boldly advocating any policy the management may propose. Their doing so may endanger their investment; but as their holdings are probably small, the loss will be easily wiped out by the reversion of some coveted office. These are the persons who, earlier in their career, say " hush " when some bold shareholder calls in question the proceedings of the board, and generally act as if a position of opposition to the executive were " flat blasphemy ". Strange as it may seem, it is nevertheless unfortunately too true that, except when a company has got avowedly into a quagmire, any one who presumes to raise a warning voice is rigorously put down, not so much by the board's direct action as by the attitude of these bloodsuckers. The success which attends their proceedings is due, doubtless, in many cases, to the impolitic, unprepared, and excited manner in which many worthy shareholders manage to involve themselves, when they are making a probably well-deserved attack. The weaknesses in the case, as presented under such circumstances, are skilfully taken advantage of by the emergency men ; and at the same time estrange those who would otherwise support the dissentient shareholder. But in any case, it usually comes about that the approval of the board's policy is secured, not at the hands of the *bonâ fide* shareholders, but of those who are not personally much concerned whether the company sinks or swims.

What, then, is to be done to secure that thoroughly independent auditors be appointed ? While we do not expect a cure for the existing evils, until the millennium enables the financial leopard to get rid of his spots and lie down with the kid, it would be simple enough to devise legislative methods for improving the conditions under which auditors are elected. Of course, if shareholders are absolutely determined not to attend to their own interests, the legislature cannot force them to do so. But it should at least make the conditions as suitable for securing safety as experience may show to be desirable. One excellent provision would be that, during the election of auditors, all directors and officials of the company (the chairman, perhaps, excepted) should leave the room in which the meeting was being held. Many shareholders would take part in the proceedings under such circumstances, who otherwise would remain interested but silent spectators. Again, a maximum number of years during which it would be legal for an auditor to hold office should be fixed. This change of *personnel* would, in many cases, be highly beneficial. Then the suggestion of names of auditors in the annual report should be forbidden. When a shareholder reads the following clause in the report, " The auditors, Messrs. Gullible Brothers, retire at this time, but being eligible, offer themselves for re-election," he simply regards their reappointment as secured, and thinks no more about the matter. If, however, it were illegal to mention any name in connection with the announcement that the election of auditors would form part of the business, a very different state of matters might ensue. The office would then be open to competition, without violation of professional etiquette. These provisions would not absolutely prevent unsatisfactory auditing, but they would tend very materially towards the improvement of the conditions under which auditing is at present conducted.

CHAPTER XIV.

THE DEATH OF COMPANIES.*

"Man makes a Death,
Which Nature never made."
—YOUNG.

THE term "company" includes so many varieties of associations of human beings that, while the predicate of our title might doubtless be more or less aptly applied to them all, it is expedient to define its use on the present occasion, so as to put suitable bounds to our disquisition. In a paper devoted to the interests of banking men, the phase which falls most naturally to be considered is that of profit-earning joint-stock corporations; and it is as relative to such companies that the following remarks are intended.

Death, the termination of manifest sentient existence, is an absolute law of the animal world; and decay is probably predominant in all material creation. But corporations are not subject to the conditions either of animal life or of inanimate creations, being under purely abstract conditions, and having existence and personality only as legal fictions. And yet we find that, notwithstanding their inherent right, both as regards their theoric and legal conditions, to perpetual succession (not to speak of a common

* Published in 1895.

seal), they manifest a decided moribund tendency. We are not aware that the vital statistics of companies have as yet been systematically investigated, but there seems to be no reason to doubt that profit-earning joint-stock companies have not yet exhibited greater degrees of longevity than the animal creation. Corporations other than those of the profit-earning variety do indeed exceed in life-record any known instances of the duration of animal life; but those of which we are treating can hardly do more than rival the elephant or the parrot, the alligator or the Aldabra tortoise, while no corporation of any kind can show instances of longevity equal to those exhibited by the vegetable kingdom.

It may be said that the mortality of companies is merely incidental to their relationship to mortal humanity —that all man's material creations wear out by use, while his immaterial suffer from the evils adherent to his own conditions. But this is only arguing in a circle—at best it is but a truism, and does not help us to solve the problem. Why do companies (like the flowers) die? The Bank of England and the Bank of Scotland are probably the oldest business corporations extant, and they have just completed two centuries of existence. But had they been founded by William the Conqueror and Malcolm Canmore, their continued existence would not have been abnormal, however surprising it might have been from its singularity. We may be sure their perpetual succession would have had as little perpetuity as their common seals, which would undoubtedly have been used towards securing the perpetual succession of some royal or noble thief. The banks would either have been robbed and murdered, or they would have committed suicide as is so common with companies still. But this would all have been incidental to the circumstances in which they were placed—not involved in the principle of corporate existence which contemplates a continuance as perpetual as the precession of the equinoxes.

It is a somewhat extraordinary fact that, notwithstanding this unconditional claim to immortality, the history of companies should exhibit an almost identical experience with that of mortal humanity, from and even prior to birth onwards to the grave. Some companies are still-born, and many are quick-born which should never have seen the light of day. Some are diseased from their conception; while some, born healthily and respectably, fall away and become reprobates. Others grow to full age only to become the victims of misfortune. Robbery and murder, often by professing friends, and despairing suicide terminate the career of many; while, were it not that " corporations have neither souls to be saved nor bodies to be kicked," the iniquities, cruelties, and selfishness which characterise the proceedings of many would justify their condign punishment both here and hereafter. Some are rash, some are extravagant, some overbold, and some too timid. It is, however, pleasing to be able to reflect that, as with humanity, so with companies; a few live respectable and useful lives in credit and renown. It may even be that, as the vital statistics of mankind show a tendency towards lengthened periods of existence, so companies may in future times improve on their past record.

There is another aspect in which corporate existence bears a striking resemblance to the lives of mankind. As each human being has a life peculiarly his own, into which no one enters, or can enter, an unknown innocence or an unknown guilt, with various degrees of combination of both, so with companies, the inner life differs materially from that which the annual chapter of autobiography details. This is so not only with moribund companies, but even with those which are in the most robust corporate health. If one of those clever fellows, of whom there are so many now-a-days, would discover financial Röntgen rays for application to corporate bodies, the resulting anatomical study would be highly interesting and instructive to shareholders, and stock exchange prices would rule lower.

That the so-called great Napoleon, notwithstanding the outstanding characteristics of his career, had many contemptible weaknesses and meannesses is made evident by the narrative of his great friend and worshipper, the Duchesse d'Abrantes. But he had one quality, among those which made him distinguished, without which all would have gone for little. He was pre-eminently a reader of character; he could readily tell who were the most suitable men for the various appointments he had to make; he could read the mind, the face, the body; and, unscrupulous as he was himself, he could recognise and appreciate the higher qualities in others, or detect the deceit or selfishness which lurked behind their specious phrases. This power, however, is comparatively rare—many persons think they have it, but conceit, a quality incompatible with greatness, strangles it in its birth; or self-sufficiency prevents that cultivation of the faculty which is necessary to its perfecting, or selfishness makes indifferent to it. To this want is due in many cases the death of companies whose careers might have been indefinitely prolonged. The injudicious appointments of one generation continue far into the next; and the damage done, even when recognised, will hardly be remedied before its close. Thus a business which, it may be, has been laboriously built up through generations of careful management, may, in a few years, be sent rolling on the down grade, whose bottom is death.

It is a great misfortune that, in the business world, the higher virtues handicap their exponents as competitors in the battle of life. Selfishness, that one great sin of humanity which is the parent of all the others, though allied with ignorance, is more potent than altruism combined with knowledge. The world, like the Kingdom of Heaven, is taken by storm; and the man who pushes his neighbour aside, whether it be by the knock-down direct, the secret detraction, or the gentle elbowing process, is the one that his fellows crown with honour, riches and power. Thus it too often happens that the fate of a company lies in the hands of men whose ideas of duty recognise it solely as a means to their aggrandisement and glorification. It may be feared that, less and less, does management identify its own and a company's interests. Not, perhaps, that this is consciously done to a greater extent than formerly, but, under more realistic and less pretentious conditions, men involuntarily combined the personal and the official *rôles*. Thus the most is made of the present, the future being left to take care of itself; the reserve of strength which might secure a green old age is drawn on to make a present display; and present prosperity, which, stored up, would bid defiance to the adversity which is sure to come, is availed of for present gratification. People cannot both eat their cake and have it. In this, not utilitarian, but selfish age people prefer to eat it.

One of the most common causes which lead to the death of companies is the neglect of the teaching of experience. We do not refer to personal experience, that still enforces itself on the pupil, as it has proverbially done since time immemorial. *Experientia docet stultos.* But the study of the past, the profiting by the experience of those who have trodden the way of life before us, is neglected in this self-sufficient age. Modern conceit acknowledges no teacher; it is sublime in its self-reliance, yet it is Brummagem ware to the pride of the past, which it would fain eclipse. The modern is all-knowing in his self-esteem, thinking that his cursory reading has taught him all he can learn from the past; yet, as we have been taught from infancy, there is nothing new under the sun. This is as true in regard to companies as of human beings. Details change, the outward manifestations and conditions alter from time to time, but the essential principles are ever the same. There is uniformity in nature, both in the comparison of different ages of the world's history, and in the comparison of different departments of life of the same age. Thus the company that would see long days must, like the men whose creation it is, live soberly in self-restraint, recognising that every effort of over-exertion or self-indulgence is simply a draft against the balance of its vitality; while prudent economy of energy secures a provision against the contingencies of the future.

APPENDIX A.

Average Rates of DISCOUNT charged for BILLS on London at three months' currency; of INTEREST charged on CASH ACCOUNTS; and of INTEREST allowed on DEPOSIT RECEIPTS by the banks in Scotland, from 1865-1896, inclusive.

Year.	Bill Rate.		Cash Account Rate.		Deposit Receipt Rate.	
	Annual. Per Cent.	Decade. Per Cent.	Annual. Per Cent.	Decade. Per Cent.	Annual. Per Cent.	Decade. Per Cent.
1864 - - -	7·35		7·27		4·10	
1865 - - -	4·76	6·06	5·52	6·40	3·57	3·84 (2 yrs.).
1866 - - -	6·69		7·07		4·33	
1867 - - -	3·05		4·82		2·05	
1868 - - -	3		4·50		2	
1869 - - -	3·30		4·64		2·26	
1870 - - -	3·22		4·64		2·20	
1871 - - -	3·29		4·71		2·30	
1872 - - -	4·08		5·24		2·97	
1873 - - -	4·78		5·73		3·53	
1874 - - -	3·74		5·02		2·70	
1875 - - -	3·41	3·86	4·82	5·12	2·40	2·67
1876 - - -	3·30		4·69		2·30	
1877 - - -	3·34		4·72		2·35	
1878 - - -	3·97		5·19		2·86	
1879 - - -	3·12		4·72		3·46	
1880 - - -	3		4·76		2	
1881 - - -	3·63		5·08		2·50	
1882 - - -	4·14		5·51		2·87	
1883 - - -	3·58		5·06		2·54	
1884 - - -	3·36		4·90		2·30	
1885 - - -	3·38	3·48	4·83	4·95	2·27	2·54
1886 - - -	3·37		4·85		1·97	
1887 - - -	3·63		4·93		2·20	
1888 - - -	3·58		5·03		2·26	
1889 - - -	3·69		5·13		2·20	
1890 - - -	4·57		5·61		2·91	
1891 - - -	3·48		4·96		1·93	
1892 - - -	3·04		4·73		1·53	
1893 - - -	3·34		4·88		1·76	
1894 - - -	3		4·54		1·50	
1895 - - -	2·53	3·42	4·50	4·92	1·04	1·93
1896 - - -	2·99		4·63		1·33	
1897 - - -	2·96	to 9th Sep.	4·70		1·31	
Gen. Avergs.	3·70		5·05		2·41	

Note.—The average D.R. rate for the ten years 1856-65 was 2·78 per cent.; but, from 1858-60, the Clydesdale Bank allowed at first ¼ per cent. and latterly ⅛ per cent. more, on deposits at one month's notice.

APPENDIX B.

Note Issues of the Scottish Banks.

Banks Issuing under the Act of 1845.	Authorised Issues.			Average Issues.	
	1845.	1857.	1863-4.	1882-3.	1883-4.
Bank of Scotland	£300,485	£343,418	£372,148	£868,190	£1,079,041
Royal Bank of Scotland	183,000	216,451	502,974	798,229	927,342
British Linen Company	438,024	438,024	491,703	656,305	853,682
Dundee Banking Company	33,451	(to Royal)	46,259	—	—
Perth Banking Company	38,656	(to Union)	—	—	—
Banking Company in Aberdeen	88,467	Do.	—	—	—
Commercial Bank of Scotland	374,880	374,880	537,840	793,413	929,451
National Bank of Scotland	297,024	297,024	454,375	659,768	827,044
Aberdeen Town and County Banking Company	70,133	70,133	135,446	212,413	303,700
Union Bank of Scotland	327,223	454,346	592,519	809,511	950,772
Ayrshire Banking Company	53,656	*(lapsed)	—	—	—
Western Bank of Scotland	281,282	Do.	—	—	—
Central Bank of Scotland	42,933	(to B. of S.)	59,450	—	—
North of Scotland Banking Company	154,319	154,319	205,373	383,363	438,640
Clydesdale Banking Company	101,028	274,321	368,850	573,171	715,651
Caledonian Banking Company	53,434	53,434	72,169	100,172	132,351
Eastern Bank of Scotland	33,636	(†to Clyde)	—	—	—
City of Glasgow Bank	72,921	(lapsed)	357,581	—	—
Edinburgh and Glasgow Bank	136,657	(to Clyde)	—	—	—
Totals	**£3,087,209**	**£2,676,350**	**£4,296,687**	**£5,854,565**	**£7,157,683**

(Present names at page 169.)   * Through Western.   † Through Edinburgh and Glasgow.

APPENDIX C.

THE BANK OF ENGLAND AND SILVER.

As these sheets are preparing for the press, comes the announcement of the Bank of England's surrender to the Silverites. The seriousness of this action cannot readily be exaggerated. The old lady of Threadneedle Street has often been abused for tardiness in taking up new ideas. But, partly on account of her rigid adherence to established principles, she has hitherto been regarded with undoubting confidence, not only as regards inherent strength, but also as the guardian of that foundation of British credit, the ultimate reserve of the embodiment of the recognised standard of value, gold. No financial heresies have previously found a home in the bank parlour; and the British public and bankers have been content to let the bimetallists rage and adjust, and readjust, their hopeless schemes for joining the two metals in an unnatural alliance, safe in the conviction that they could always get gold, or gold value, when they required it. They have been rudely awakened from their dream of safety, and find that there is danger of the gold reserve being debased with an admixture of one-fifth of silver. Fortunately the Bank of England does not now occupy the commanding position it once did, so that when it essays to use its still giant strength in imitating Samson's final feat, the joint-stock banks are potent enough to restrain it. The resolute action of the London Clearing bankers in opposing the scheme has been received with a sense of relief. The bank is, no doubt, empowered to act as it proposes, but it must begin to realise that it has a host to reckon with.

While it may thus be inferred that there is little actual danger of the proposal being carried out, the action of the bank has been of a very unfortunate character. That it has put heart of grace into the Silverites is the least part of the damage done. The instillation of doubt into men's minds as to the absolute permanence of our gold standard is in itself a calamity which only time, and steady adherence to sound money doctrines, will counteract. Fortunately, general banking opinion in the United Kingdom is sound on the question, and, as we have seen, that opinion is capable of enforcing itself.

APPENDIX D.

Official Names, Nature of Constitutions, and Details and Market Value of Capital, of the Banks of Issue in Scotland.

Names.	Head Offices.	Constitution.	Capital.					
			Division.	Paid.	Callable.		Value 30th Oct., 1897.
					For Business.	For Liquidation.	
							Per cent.
The Governor and Company of the Bank of Scotland	Edinburgh	Act of Parliament	Stock £150	£100	£50	—	367
The Royal Bank of Scotland	Do.	Royal Charter and Act of Parliament	Do. 100	100	—	—	235
The British Linen Company	Do.	Royal Charter	Do. 100	100	—	—	475
The Commercial Bank of Scotland, Limited	Do.	Royal Charter and Companies Acts	Shares 100	20	40	£40	430$\frac{5}{8}$
The National Bank of Scotland, Limited	Do.		Stock 500	100	100	300	405
The Union Bank of Scotland, Limited	Glasgow and Edinburgh	Contract of Copartnery and Companies Acts	Shares 50	10	—	40	246$\frac{7}{8}$
The Clydesdale Bank, Limited	Glasgow		Do. 50	10	—	40	227$\frac{1}{4}$
Town and County Bank, Limited	Aberdeen		Do. 35	7	13	15	314$\frac{1}{4}$
North of Scotland Bank, Limited	Do.		Do. 20	4	4	12	249$\frac{3}{4}$
Caledonian Banking Company, Limited	Inverness		Do. 12$\frac{1}{2}$	2$\frac{1}{2}$	2$\frac{1}{2}$	7$\frac{1}{2}$	185

INDEX.

ACCEPTANCES, 19, 34, 118.
Advances, 22, 25, 36, 119-23.
Agents, 106, 128, 137.
Aikman, A., 53.
Anderson, G., 63.
Auditing, 153.

BALANCE-SHEETS, 15-28.
Bank buildings, 26-28, 38.
— customers, 107.
— offices, 30.
— officers, 104, 112.
— of England, 12, 101, 167.
— of Mona, 67.
— of Scotland, 46, 47.
— profits, 6, 42.
— reports, vii., 2, 46-67.
Banker, old Scottish, 103-4.
Bankers' exchange, 117.
Banking, viii., 1, 8.
— local, 106.
— study of, 130, 135.
Banks established, 2, 15.
— experience, 3, 8.
— governmental tone, 108.
— relative positions, 41, 77, 169.
— Scottish in England, 13.
Baring Bros. & Co., 12.
Blyth, R., 57.
Branches, 29, 39, 105, 125.
— and profits, 71-4.
British Linen Co., 2, 50-1.
Brodie, P., 51.

CALEDONIAN Bank, 64-5.
Canvassing, 132.
Capital, 6, 19-23, 35, 112, 169.
Cash accounts, 120, 126.
Character, knowledge of, 161.
City of Glasgow Bank, 11, 66-7, 82.
Clearing house, 124.
Clydesdale Bank, 58-9.
Cochrane, T., 61.
Collie, A., & Co., 12.
Commercial Bank of Scotland, 52-3.
Companies, 158.
Credit, 85, 92.

Crises, 11, 12.
Cunningham, J. M., 59.
Currency, 98.

DAVIDSON, D., 47.
Deposits, 15, 16, 33, 76, 113.
Discount rates, 165.
Dividends, 46-66, 76.
Drafts, 19, 34, 118.
Duncan, W. J., 55.

ESSARS, Pierre des, 111.
Experience, viii., 32, 46-67, 163.

FIDDES, E., 63.
Findlater, J., 61.
Fleming, J. S., 49.
Forgeries, 47.
François, G., v.
Future, the, 80, 109.

GAIRDNER, C., 57, 96.
Glasgow banks, 2.
Glasgow Herald, vii.
Gold reserve, 92-102, 167.
— scarcity of, 97.

HERITABLE property, 26-8, 38, 123.
Hotson, H. A., 51.
Huie, D. R. W., 49.

INSTITUTE of Bankers in Scotland, viii., 148.
Interest rates, 9, 165.
Investment companies, 85.

LITTLEJOHN, W., 61.
London and Westminster Bank, 12, 84.
Losses, 42, 78, 82, 84.
Lumsden, R., 63.

MACMILLAN, E. H., 65.
Mackenzie, A. K., 53.

NATIONAL Bank of Scotland, 54-5.
North of Scotland Bank, 62-3.

www.ingramcontent.com/pod-product-compliance
Lightning Source LLC
Chambersburg PA
CBHW020246170426
43202CB00008B/252